I0006728

For further information:
SBBI Publishing, Inc.
406 Broadway
Los Angeles, CA. 90401
www.sbbipublishing.com

Library of Congress Cataloging-in-Publication Data
Larson, Garr, 1963 -
Understand Social Selling...Or Fail / Garr Larson
        p. cm
ISBN 978-0-578-10845-2
1. Internet marketing 2. Electronic commerce
I. Larson, Garr, 1963 – II. Title

Printed in the United States of America

10 9 8 7 6 5 4 3 2

UNDERSTAND SOCIAL SELLING...

by
Garr Larson

For Neethy, Priya and Rory, who lived through all the close finishes with support, love and a whole lot (a whole lot!) of laughter. Pepper, Nutmeg, and now Bodhi helped too.

WELCOME TO THE OR FAIL SERIES!

You're not a Dummy or a Complete Idiot.

We won't treat you like one.

The **OR FAIL** series is designed to be a small book that delivers a big impact on your life – **NOW**!

You want answers fast. To succeed, you need to understand the most important changes happening in our world today…and you have precious little time to do so.

OR FAIL is designed to deliver clear insight on the issues that today's executive faces, and provide you with actions you can take the moment you stop reading. This **OR FAIL** book will give you a path, process and a point of view you can choose to pursue by the time the flight staff says "buh-bye now" at the door on a normal non-stop flight.

Need more? Each book is full of online links to every tool, tutorial and update you'll need to make change happen fast.

Seek, Learn, Grow...Or Fail™

WELCOME TO THE OR FAIL SERIES v

TABLE OF CONTENTS vi

VISUAL TABLE OF CONTENTS. x

20 SECOND INTRO. xiii

TWO-MINUTE INTRO xv

PART ONE

WHAT IS SOCIAL SELLING 3
SOCIAL SELLING IS NOT NEW, BUT... 4
TYPES OF SOCIAL SELLING: YOU FIND IT,
      WE FIND IT, IT FINDS YOU 6
WHAT WE TRUST NOW. 16
THE SOLUTION IS EASY!. 19
OUT WITH THE OLD, IN WITH THE NEW
      (SALES FUNNEL THAT IS) 20
TAKE ACTION NOW! 23
3 THINGS NOT TO DO 25
NEXT - SOCIAL SELLING FUNNEL 26

PART TWO

THE NEW SOCIAL SALES FUNNEL 27
SOLUTION? SEED, FEED AND LEAD™! 29
SEED = LISTEN 37
    KNOW WHO TO LISTEN TO

FEED = ENGAGE 39
    KNOW WHERE TO ENGAGE
LEAD = COMPEL. 41
    KNOW HOW TO COMPEL

PART THREE

HOW TO SEED: YOUR STEP-BY-STEP GUIDE 43
SEED STEP ONE: LISTEN TO YOUR CUSTOMERS. 45
CREATE YOUR ONLY STATEMENT 46
LISTEN TO WHAT YOUR CUSTOMERS SEARCH FOR 50
THE $10 MILLION DOLLAR CUP OF COFFEE 56
LISTEN TO THOSE THAT HAVE INFLUENCE. 61
FIND YOUR FIVE 63
SEED STEP TWO: LISTEN TO YOUR COMPETITION 68
FOLLOW THE MONEY TRAIL. 71
FIND YOUR FIVE 72
SEED STEP THREE: TODAYS SEEDING TOOLS 76

PART FOUR

HOW TO FEED: YOUR STEP-BY-STEP GUIDE 85
FEED STEP ONE: KNOW WHERE TO ENGAGE 87
BACK TO THE FUTURE – THE MCCOURT SCALE 88
PRIORITIAZE YOUR TOP 3 SOCIAL
      SELLING SITES. 92
FEED STEP TWO: RULES OF ENGAGEMENT. 97

TO BE TRULY ENGAGING, YOU JUST NEED
    TO BE G.R.E.A.T 99
ENGAGING CONTENT IS USEFUL AND UNIQUE. 106
FEED STEP THREE: ENGAGE WITH
    THE RIGHT TOOLS 110

PART FIVE

HOW TO LEAD: YOUR STEP-BY-STEP GUIDE 119
LEAD STEP ONE: TELL COMPELLING STORIES 121
STORIES ARE WHO WE ARE (ALL OF US). 121
CREATE A COMPELLING STORY. YOURS!. 124
MAKE YOUR STORY YOUR MOVIE:
    IT'S AS EASY AS 1-2-3 129
GREAT S.T.O.R.I.E.S MAKE GREAT BLOCKBUSTERS. . . . 139
DON'T FORGET THE TRAILERS. 143
LEAD STEP TWO: OFFER COMPELLING
    PROMOTIONS 147
YOUR CALEDAR OF EVENTS. 148
WHAT MAKES A GREAT PROMOTION? 149
COMPELLING, AND PROVEN PROMOTIONS. 152
LEAD STEP THREE: COMPEL WITH
    THE RIGHT TOOLS 160

PART SIX

MEASURE YOUR SUCCESS WITH SOCIAL
SELLING METRICS 167

A WARNING ABOUT SOCIAL SELLING METRICS...... 168

FIRST, USE S.M.A.R.T METRICS 169

THE TOP TEN SOCIAL SELLING METRICS (OK, 9) 172

WHICH METRICS? IT'S AS EASY AS

    TICK, TACK, TRACK! 175

BEST SOCIAL SELLING METRIC TOOLS 178

PART SEVEN

EXCLUSIVE FIRST LOOK AT FACEBOOK'S

    WANT BUTTON! 183

A BIT OF "LIKE" HISTORY 184

NOT EVOLUTION, BUT REVOLTION 185

THE POWER OF WANT 187

10 REASONS TO WANT THE WANT BUTTON 189

WHAT TO DO NOW 194

FINAL THOUGHTS 198

100% GUARANTEED! 199

ACKNOWLEDGEMENTS........................... 200

ABOUT THE AUTHOR 200

ABOUT THE CREATIVE DIRECTOR.................. 201

WANT TO WRITE FOR OR FAIL? 201

1 PART ONE

Social selling "...is using social media in the context of retail".

3 types of social selling: You Find It, We Find It, It Finds You.

We trust opinions, reviews, and recommendations of others...not marketers

The New Social Sales Funnel!

2 PART TWO

How do you sell socially? Easy!

SEED, FEED, AND LEAD™

SEED = Know who to LISTEN to

FEED = Know where to ENGAGE

LEAD = Know how to Compel your customer to purchase

3 PART THREE

Your step by step SEED guide:

Step One: Learn to listen to your CUSTOMER

Find your Top 5 influencers

Step Two: Learn to listen to your COMPETITION

Step Three: A review of todays seeding TOOLS

4 PART FOUR

Your step by step FEED guide:

Step One: Learn WHERE to engage

Your Top 3 social selling sites

Step Two: Learn the RULES of engagement

G. R. E. A. T. content

Step Three: Engage with the right TOOLS

5 PART FIVE

Your step by step LEAD guide

Step One: Learn to tell compelling stories.

Make your story a movie. It's as easy as 1, 2, 3!

Step Two: Learn to offer compelling promotions

Step Three: Learn to compel with the right tools

6 PART SIX

Measure success with social selling metrics

First, use S.M.A.R.T. metrics

Top 10 metrics to use (o.k., 9)

Which metrics? It's as easy as Tick, Tack, Track!

7 PART SEVEN

Exclusive look at Facebook's WANT button

What you want... is WANT

A bit of "Like" history

Not evolution, but revolution

Top 10 reasons to put the WANT button to work for you

What you can do now

8 YOU'RE DONE!

FINAL THOUGHTS

Get your free certificate of education!

More resources at ORFAIL.com

ACKNOWLEDGEMENTS

ABOUT US

WANT TO WRITE FOR OR FAIL? DO IT!

An optimist is someone who goes after Moby Dick in a rowboat and takes tartar sauce with him.

- Zig Ziglar

20 SECOND INTRO

You're probably having a tough time right now. That's why you've picked up this OR FAIL book.

Whether you're a small entrepreneur, a hurried manager in charge of a large staff, a chef, or a professor – you need to know more about the massive shift in selling taking place right now.

You need to understand social selling, or you may fail.

This book will not only give you a complete understanding of the new world of social selling, but will provide clear steps to take action now, and give you online tools to help you sell more of anything using social media.

As we always say;

Small Book. Big Impact. ™

Turn the page for more…

Unless you walk out into the unknown, the odds of making a profound difference in your life are pretty low.

- Tom Peters

TWO MINUTE INTRO

Social media has changed **everything**.

Social media has created the fastest growing change to our society in history. Never has there been such a fundamental shift in our lives; How we communicate, how we work – and now, **how we sell.**

How we sell our brands, and our companies has changed. How we sell ourselves has changed. How we sell our ideas, and how we sell our theologies has changed.

Have you changed how you sell?

Do you use the power of social selling to make your business stronger? Do you use it to change where you are in your career goals and where you want to be? Do you embrace it, but don't know where to start? Do you think it's too late?

Well, good news! Social selling, even with all its media coverage, promotion and sea of competitors, is still a swaddling baby in its life cycle.

You've chosen the perfect time to learn more!

In this book we will do exactly what the title says: You will understand social selling, and in turn become successful at it. You will know how to get started for yourself, how to profit, and have a better life because of it. It may sound contrite – but congratulations!

Just by picking up this book you are changing your future by taking the time to understand the simple, but profound changes that are happening in our lifetime.

We use the "OR FAIL" name of this book not as a marketing gimmick, or to sound threatening, but because we know you have a choice.

You can embrace change, understand and use it, and become an agent of change yourself…

…or you can fade into the background of your work and your community as change happens around you.

You truly can…

"Understand Social Selling...Or Fail."

Success is not final, failure is not fatal; it is the courage to continue that counts.

- *Winston Churchill*

READY TO SUCCEED AT SOCIAL SELLING?

"Seek, Learn, Grow...Or Fail" ™

Everyone lives by selling something.

- Robert Louis Stevenson

PART ONE

WHAT IS SOCIAL SELLING?

Everyone is selling something.

A better liquid soap. A new degree program at a college, or maybe a breakfast fundraiser, or car wash. You're even selling yourself when you're seeking that new job or promotion.

Today, instead of the traditional approach of printing a flyer, putting an ad in a newspaper, creating a TV or radio spot, or posting your resume to a popular job board, we are more likely to turn to social media (Facebook, Linkedin, Pinterest to name a few) to sell.

So what is social selling?

"Social selling is the use of social media, online media, and any other social forum that supports social interaction and user contributions, to assist in the online buying and selling of products and services."

Or the cocktail party version:

"Selling using social media – the use of social technologies - in the context of retail."

SOCIAL SELLING IS NOT NEW, BUT...

Ever since there has been a crowd of people, even a small crowd, there has been social selling. Social selling in our era is simply the evolution of people of similar goals and interests coming together to help each other. In generations past guilds played the same role, as did trade groups and unions. More recently business groups like Rotary, Kiwanis and local Chambers of Commerce all had the same goal – increase sales within a circle of influence.

But social selling went from evolution to revolution, as social media became an integral part of the Digital Generations life. In fact, social media has fueled a truly explosive growth in s-commerce (social commerce) – with just the daily deal portion (pioneered by Groupon) expected to reach nearly $4 billion in the next few years. An amazing fact, considering the daily deal model is just a few years old.

...IT CHANGES EVERYTHING

TOP TEN REASONS SOCIAL SELLING IS IMPORTANT - TODAY!

10 Whether you're selling socially or not, it is already part of your customer's life

9 Facebook, alone, is the world's third largest culture – with over 1 billion users and growing

8 We are social, and always have been. This part of human nature will grow, not diminish

7 Social selling can fast forward your marketing goals and is easy to learn

6 It's hard to fight the proven success of social selling, and it's getting more important every day

5 It's cheap!

4 Social selling is going mobile, which opens an even bigger opportunity for you

3 Your timing is perfect. Social selling is still just getting started!

2 It's easy to learn, and doesn't take any detailed technological skills

1 **If you don't embrace social selling... your competitors will!**

EASY GUIDE TO THE TYPES OF SOCIAL SELLING

There are hundreds (if not thousands!) of examples of social selling opportunities.

So how do we best grasp the complexity of social selling?

Easy. Lets simply look at **influence.**
It's the keystone of selling.

Someone, or something influences us when we make a purchase. Social media can have a significant influence on what we buy, and why we buy it. To categorize this influence, legendary Hollywood digital marketer and branding guru Tracy McCourt devised an easy to understand categorization of the many types of social selling opportunities by how they influence our customers. The categories include:

YOU FIND IT – Customer discovered review, information and deals.

WE FIND IT – Trusting and seeking the opinions of others in a social network to make purchasing decisions.

IT FINDS YOU – Information and deals are delivered to users for their review.

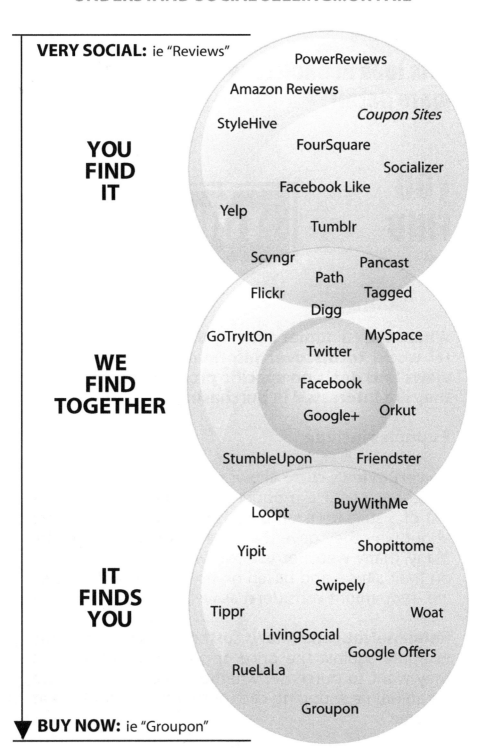

VERY SOCIAL: ie "Reviews"

YOU FIND IT

PowerReviews

Amazon Reviews

Coupon Sites

StyleHive

FourSquare

Socializer

Facebook Like

Yelp

Tumblr

Scvngr

Pancast

Path

Flickr

Tagged

Digg

WE FIND TOGETHER

GoTryItOn

MySpace

Twitter

Facebook

Google+

Orkut

StumbleUpon

Friendster

BuyWithMe

Loopt

Yipit

Shopittome

IT FINDS YOU

Swipely

Tippr

Woat

LivingSocial

Google Offers

RueLaLa

Groupon

▼ **BUY NOW:** ie "Groupon"

Lets look at each type of social selling in more detail.

YOU FIND IT

Where the customer actively digs around the digital world to discover information, feedback, reviews and deals on specific products and services they are interested in purchasing.

Examples include:

PowerReviews.com: Allows customers to share their experience with a product by ranking its success (4 out of 5 stars for example), as well as add comments about why they gave the product the rank they did. Many, many websites use software products like this on their sites – and based on how important reviews are – you might consider it as well.

RetailMeNot.com: Allows customers to find coupons to apply against the price of products and services they want to purchase, whether it's a discount code for an online shopping cart, or to print out and use at a store.

YOU FIND IT ALSO INCLUDES

Yelp.com: Allows customers to write reviews on restaurants, nightclubs, spa's and more. Yelp has done a good job monetizing this space by offering detailed information to retailers for advertising and by offering specials exclusive to yelp users. A competitor is restaurant.com, who has also grown significantly by offering users great exclusive deals.

Scvngr.com: Allows customers to participate in games that ultimately provide rewards, discounts and the opportunity to get free items. A pioneer in "alternative" social selling platforms, Scvngr has both a customer side and an institutional side, where businesses, non-profits, or any type of organization can create challenges that lead to their front doors! If you haven't already experimented with the "game meets selling" world, it's time to give it a whirl.

WE FIND IT

Where customers seek to share their everyday life experiences, to communicate, and to find information they trust from a network. While selling is a by-product of the process (not the purpose) "we find it" sites have been the birthplace of social selling.

Examples include:

Facebook.com: Obviously Facebook comes to mind first (with over a billion users) as the behemoth of social selling. But its also the case-book example of the We Find Together business model, where users trust other opinions and are heavily influenced by others who "like" products and services. Every indication is that the experience of sharing thoughts on, well, everything will become an even bigger part of Facebook with the addition of ""Want" or "Collect" buttons.

StumbleUpon.com: Allows users to "stumble" through the web almost randomly, finding interesting articles, sites and products that they may never have found otherwise. Based on subject preferences, users can "give the thumbs up" to a site they stumbled upon, and as a result the product and web pages that are "found" receive more exposure to all users.

GoTryItOn.com: Allows customers to send pictures of outfits they are interested in purchasing and get instant feedback on what others think of it. Perhaps by definition the ultimate use of We Find Together influence, savvy retailers are hosting GoTryItOn parties, and rewarding users with discounts for participating both in the stores and online.

Twongo.com: Allows customers to receive larger discounts on daily deals the more they share and promote the deal with others. By sharing, users are rewarded with additional discounts, loyalty points and access to exclusive deals in the future.

Ultimately, the **We Find It** model will migrate into one of the largest forms of social selling, especially with the advent of Facebook's "Want" or "Collect" platform, but more on that later!

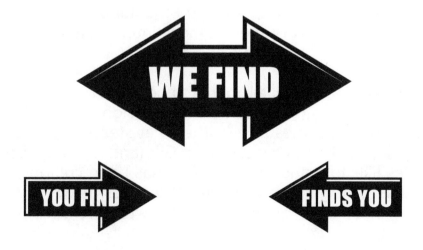

IT FINDS YOU

Where the entire purpose of the social experience is selling. Whether a customer has elected to be "told" of a deal through a daily deal site, or they like to be presented with an array of new deals on products and services, this area's focus is on presenting compelling deals constantly.

Examples include:

Groupon.com: Allows users to receive at least one, if not more, deals (that Groupon has negotiated) but are only viable for limited time frame or in limited quantities. At first, these sites focused on a delivering a broad range of deals, but over time hundreds of daily deal sites with very specific niche interests have been launched.

Gilt.com: Allows participants to be part of daily deals on collections of goods – usually designer and higher end accessories and clothes – at steep discounts. Again, the key to success with Gilt (and other similar sites like Joss and Main, or Fab) has been creating a sense of urgency around limited times in which to buy, and limited quantities available to purchase.

Roozt.com: Allows users to discover eco-friendly, trendsetting, cause-oriented brands and products. Similar to Etsy.com, in that small artisans can hawk products to many, Roozt however follows the daily deal model, and has a robust program that pays users to introduce their website to others (through a reward program).

LivingSocial.com: Allows users, similar to Groupon, to specify city deals or take advantage of a national deal each day. Recently Living Social has been gaining popularity compared to other competitors, mainly by creating more compelling savings as the number of users increases.

As of this printing, for example, Living Social offered a $10 Starbucks gift card for only $5, selling **the most Daily Deals of all time** – 1.5 million customers purchased the deal in just a few hours – selling out of all the allotted gift cards! Now that's social selling!

WHAT IS RIGHT FOR YOU?

As we begin to build your social selling plan using our step-by-step process, the right sphere of influence from the McCourt definition where you should concentrate on will become clear.

First, however, we have to **listen** carefully to where the customer is already talking about you, and who the most influential individuals are already in your market.

From this, we will discover how to **engage** your customer by participating in the same networks and websites they do.

Finally, we will learn the most effective, and profitable ways to **compel** them to use your services or buy your products.

In a way, we're sticking to all the elements of the classic "sales funnel" logic. On the other hand, never before has the customer had more interaction, participation and engagement with those they trust to influence their buying decisions.

WHAT WE TRUST NOW

Reality is, we trust the opinions of those in our social circle (even if we have never met them!) more than we do TV advertising, billboards, polls, banner ads, or anything else.

And it will change your world. Here's why:

50%

of all companies will generate sales via their social online efforts by 2015

45%

increase in online shopping expected by 2016

77%

of all online shoppers use reviews

90%

trust recommendations they get from people they know

75%

trust the recommendation of people they don't even know

77%

of shoppers like getting exclusive deals from social sites

WOULD A TEEN TRUST THAT GUY?

*" I learned the "trust" lesson well before the advent of online social selling during the **early years of Hot Topic** – the national chain of alternative and music influenced stores in practically ever mall in the US. Even though the story of Hot Topic is a classic garage to nationwide success story, we still had to create a model different than anything done before.*

Even as a small team, we knew our success would come from truly knowing our customer; their wants, their desires, and their passion to be different. The problem was gathering raw data and engaging conversations with teens when we could more easily pass for narcotics agents than insiders. Our solution was simple – and social. We reached out to our loyal and enterprising store associates and volunteered to pay for any concert ticket, club pass or any other form of related entertainment as long as we promptly got a full report on the happenings, the mood, the fashion and the influences. And information we got! Pages and pages of insights and direction that we religiously reviewed and that helped develop a retailer that not only led, but fed the needs of our customer because we were basing our offering on the recommendations and opinions of those who were going to buy. Even then, we knew creating a strategy for social selling was crucial to our success.

THE SOLUTION IS EASY!
PLANNING AND PERSERVERANCE

That title is a little like saying – "success is just hard work and intelligence", but you need to understand two very important parts that will lead to your success in social commerce: Planning and Perseverance

Planning:
Begin with the end in mind – and planning is strategy. Strategy is your game plan on how to allocate your time, energy and expenses in order to get the biggest return on all of these. We'll spend much of the rest of the book creating, honing and implementing the best plan for you! The harder part, however, is what you provide everyday – perseverance.

Perseverance:
No plan will ever come together without "stick-to-it-ness", or perseverance.

Success in social selling comes from committing to a plan, working with it everyday, learning, changing and making your goals come true. But the key word is commitment. Your customers will look to you for great content, insight into your industry, and they will engage with your brand on a much more personal level. None of this will come true, however, unless you get into the conversation and remain integrally involved every single day.

OUT WITH THE OLD, IN WITH THE NEW (SALES FUNNEL, THAT IS)

The art of selling has been written about, discussed, the-orized, packaged, taught, and reviewed perhaps more than any other single business subject in history. Selling is who we are, and what we do. Records show that man has been setting up geographic area's specific to sell-ing goods for over 150,000 years! In fact, the Greeks set up trading areas where another nation could sell their goods and called the areas Emporia's. No wonder early department stores and retail shops were called Empo-riums!

But it was in 1898, that we began to truly understand and measure the emotional journey every person takes when we buy.

Elias St. Elmo Lewis (inducted into the Advertising Hall of Fame in 1951 after his death in 1948) was an Ameri-can advertising and sales pioneer, who knew the sci-ence (and art) of selling needed a practical sales tool.

Lewis believed that the most successful salespeople fol-lowed a hierarchical process using the cognitive phas-es that buyers follow when they make a purchase. The process was outlined in his famous AIDA (which stands for Awareness, Interest, Desire and Action) sales fun-nel, which created an easy to understand, systemic ap-proach to selling a product or service. You've probably seen it time and time again in school, in lectures, and even in your workplace.

Iterations, changes, updates, improvements, and refine-ments have been made to Lewis' funnel over the past

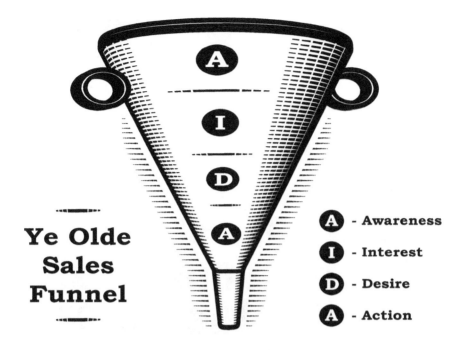

Ye Olde Sales Funnel

A - Awareness
I - Interest
D - Desire
A - Action

110 years – but they have all spoken to the same process, same approach, and same expected outcome.

Social selling changes that.

For the first time in over a century, the advertising and marketing industry, manufacturers, executives, and small business owners (everyone, in other words!) have realized that the power of social selling has made it necessary to adjust the very foundation of how we sell in order to be successful at business in the future.

That's why social selling is a revolution, not really an evolution, of how we sell now.

Let's take a minute to take a deep breath, ponder, believe, and dream! A whole new world is on your horizon. Its time to embrace it for sure, but most of all its time to **take action!**

There are one hundred and ninety nine ways to get beat, but only one way to win; get there first.

- *Willie Shoemaker*

TAKE ACTION NOW..OR FAIL. YOUR 3 X 3 TO DO LIST.

PART ONE - YOUR 3 X 3 TAKE ACTION STEPS!

ACTION	COST	BIG IMPACT!
STEP ONE: GET IN! Sign up for the top five social sites for selling, including FACEBOOK, TWITTER AND PINTEREST - and 2 others from the McCourt Chart	**$0**	Congrats! You've just entered the world of social selling... We're off and running!
STEP TWO: CHECK OUT THE COMPETITION! Make a list of bookmarks of the social media sites and social selling efforts of your top 5 competitors	**$0**	Study what your competition, peers (and therefore your customers) are doing in social selling. Any of them selling through Facebook? Using Groupon? Check them out - because by the end of this book you'll be doing more social selling than them!
STEP THREE: BUY SOMETHING! Buy anything using a social selling site today!	**You Decide**	Throw yourself into it - by simply buying something you would buy anyway socially. Use Facebook to find a new restaurant, buy a Google Offer for 50% on a new dog collar. The goal is to experience the entire start to finish social selling cycle!

There are two kinds of people, those who do the work and those who take the credit. Try to be in the first group; there is less competition there.

- Indira Gandhi

3 THINGS NOT TO DO

DON'T SPEND ANY MONEY – YET!

There are lots of sites that will want to sell you "short-cuts" to jump into social selling. But the social sites that will generate the most sales for you are free. Get to know them, and the basics of social selling first – then you can decide if any social selling services are right for you.

DON'T WAIT!

The time is now to understand social selling, and jump into it. The changes just around the corner (we'll talk about the AMAZING future of social selling later on) are starting NOW!

DON'T WORRY!

Good information, great advice, and lots of expert input is available from all over the world. Sign up for some blogs, reach out to start-up companies in the social selling space, start communicating today and you'll be an expert faster than you think! Remember – an expert is simply a person who knows more than the person sitting next to them. Of course you can start at **www.orfail.com.** We'd love to meet you and we try to have just about the best library of information and education anywhere!

NEXT - SOCIAL SELLING FUNNEL

Everything changes.
Everything stays the same.

It's true of the classic sales funnel we just got to know.

In today's selling world, having a customer concentric, service oriented, quality assured product (whether it's how you teach your class as a professor, how you manage your soccer team, or if you're selling mouse traps) will be the cornerstone of your success.

The new social selling sales funnel simply addresses how you listen to the conversations online that are important and can convert to sales, how you engage those conversations, and ultimately how you lead those conversations.

Ready for part two? You're about to learn how to Seed, Feed and Lead™ in Social Selling!

Lets go!

PART TWO

THE NEW SOCIAL SELLING FUNNEL

EVERYONE IS SELLING SOMETHING, SOCIALLY.

In the old world (up until about 2005 – real old huh?) customers followed the classic sales funnel purchase journey by gathering a large set of consideration points (features, benefits, price, quality and the like) and narrowed their final purchase choice from advertising, conversations and (whether they want to admit it or not) from emotion. Advertisers fought to "push" their way into the thought process anywhere they could. Magazines, newspapers, billboards, radio, television, sides of cars and blimps, tee shirts. You name it; We (advertisers) tried it. One of our most successful campaigns came from wrapping Volkswagen Beetles in vinyl to make them look like warthogs (our company mascot at the time). Even though they were awfully scary looking in anyone's rear view mirror, we were amazed on how many times we were asked to be in parades, to take patrons to proms, to show up at birthday parties, and more!

Today's marketing, however, is a mix of classic "push" advertising (where we try to be an integral part of the decision making process), combined with ways to allow the customer journey to also include "pull" advertising. This allows today's customer, (who we already knows trusts others more than the seller) to have a much wider consideration "net" of information available to them as they "pull" information from a variety of sources, many of which are now social.

Getting to know the process, and knowing how to master it, will lead to your success in social selling.

The good news? Its easy!

First we need to understand the New Social Selling Funnel.

Then we Seed, Feed and Lead™ our way to Success.

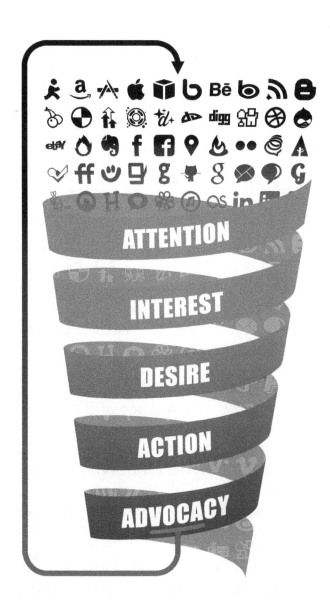

Seeding, Feeding and Leading™ Social selling is simply the process of finding ongoing conversations, engaging in them, providing content that customers want and need, and then turning all this work into an influential position for your product or service.

The Seed, Feed, Lead ™ *(ok – it's our trademark, you get it, so we'll stop putting the little "™" after every time we say it)* process is nothing more than an easy to follow, proven process to gain influence and brand engagement in your social selling efforts - fast.

The best part? The New Social Selling Funnel IS Seeding, Feeding and Leading!

When you Seed (and you learn who to listen to) you are interacting with your customers during the Attention and Interest phases of the Funnel. You'll find who has influence at the very beginning of your customers purchasing journey. And you'll discover the best way to channel Attention and Interest into Desire!

When you Feed (and you learn where to engage with your customer) you create a place and space for your brand to interact with customers on an authentic level; Truly fulfilling the needs they believe will solve the obstacles or roadblocks that hinder their success.

Finally, when you Lead (and you learn to compel your customer to purchase) you've created a Call to Action that is the culmination of your social selling efforts. You will create loyal fans that act as Advocates, broadcasting your accolades a crossed the sea of social networks!

SEED

FEED

LEAD

There is only one way to get anybody to do anything. And that is by making the other person want to do it.

- Dale Carnegie

SEED =
LISTEN

FEED =
ENGAGE

LEAD =
COMPEL

"Always do your best. What you plant now, you will harvest later.

- *Og Mandino*

SEED =
KNOW **WHO** TO LISTEN TO

FEED =
KNOW **WHERE** TO ENGAGE

LEAD =
KNOW **HOW** TO COMPEL

The best way to understand people is to listen to them.

- Ralph Nichols

SEED = LISTEN

KNOW WHO TO LISTEN TO.

Find the right conversations to grow, and the most influential people.

Seeding is the discovery phase – listening in on the right conversations, defining individuals that have significant input (influence) already in these conversations, and deciding where you are going to spend your time feeding and leading your social selling efforts.

We all are pressed for time, and expect great things from our social commerce work, so finding the perfect forums, blogs, pages and circles will be crucial to your long term success.

If you can once engage whatever is a person's prevailing passion, you need not fear what their reason can do against you.

- Lord Chesterfield

FEED = ENGAGE

KNOW WHERE TO ENGAGE.

Know the most effective places and ways to get your product or service into the conversation.

Feeding is the engagement phase – creating a place and space for your brands loyal customers to interact, to find new customers, to "land the big ones" through your leading efforts, and in general create a brand presence in the most import online venues. Feeding is having a content plan, being creative, following trends, inserting yourself and your brand into the lives of your customers and the concerns that are important to them right now.

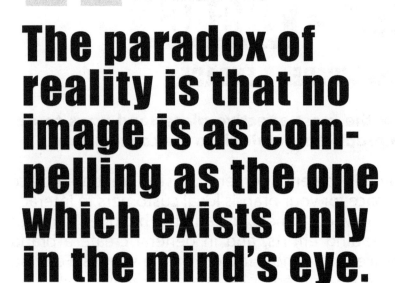

The paradox of reality is that no image is as compelling as the one which exists only in the mind's eye.

- Shana Alexander

LEAD = COMPEL

KNOW HOW TO COMPEL.

You know the Who and Where of Social Selling...here's How to compel them to buy.

Leading is the selling phase – it is taking advantage of all the hard work you have done to seed conversations and feed conversations. Leading is the most fun, it's the most rewarding, and it's the most creative part of the entire Seed, Feed, Lead process. An example of leading the conversation is creating flash sales (sales with a very limited time online) for your product or having a contest. It's working with other companies or individuals to meet a shared goal. It's getting Facebook "likes", and it's getting a million hits on YouTube.

Sounds easy enough (and it is!), but it helps to go through the process and steps we've used over the years with amazing success.

SEED =
KNOW **WHO** TO **LISTEN TO**

PART THREE

HOW TO SEED:
YOUR STEP-BY-STEP GUIDE

Successful social selling starts with not you, but **WHO.**
Who is your customer? Who is passionate about what
you do? Who is influential? The answers are the keystone's of social selling. We can answer them using our
3 easy seeding steps:

STEP ONE:
LISTEN TO YOUR CUSTOMERS

STEP TWO:
LISTEN TO YOUR COMPETITION

STEP THREE:
LISTEN WITH THE RIGHT TOOLS

HEY!

You might find it helpful to go to

www.orfail.com/seedsteps

and download all the seeding steps in an easy to use document format.

(Aren't we nice?)

SEED STEP ONE:
LISTEN TO YOUR CUSTOMER.

WHO IS YOUR TARGET AUDIENCE?

WHO ARE YOU RELEVANT TO?

You know your customer. Or, at the very least, you probably have a pretty good concept of who they are. But to truly know whom you are relevant to, it's worth the time to narrowly define your prospects.

Marty Neumeier, brilliant branding guru and author of Zag states *"...the biggest winner is not the brand that's first into the marketplace, but the one that's first into people's minds."*

Your goal then, is to be the first in people's minds - and use social selling to get there.

YOU ARE RELEVANT TO SOMEONE

Before we learn to Seed, it's important to know how your brand differentiates itself from its competitors. The same is true of any person looking for a new job, selling a home, or planning for a charity sale. What will compel someone to hire you, buy your home, or skip a ball game to come to your yard sale?

Again, we'll look to the wisdom of Mr. Neumeier for a simple exercise to find your relevancy.

"Complete the sentence:

Our brand is the ONLY _____
that _____.

If you can't keep it brief and use the ONLY, then you don't have a zag (a market differential). Your best option in that case is to make a list of competitors who could make the same claim, then start to shift your strategy away from theirs."

Whether you're a retailer, have a carpet cleaning business, or have decided to apply for that VP position at the competition, going through the process of defining your "Only" statement is a great way to start social selling. Lets look at some examples:

For a 35 store chain children's outdoor apparel retailer who wanted to sell only in locations centered in town centers (not malls):

We are the ONLY children's outdoor apparel retailer,

Who sells high quality, traditional inspired styles,

In neighborhood locations,

To parents who want their kids to live playful, balanced lives,

In an era when kids grow up too fast.

For a nationwide carpet cleaning business that embraced an eco-friendly chemical process:

We are the ONLY same day carpet cleaning service,

That uses eco-friendly alternatives to harsh chemicals, and,

Guarantees a deeper, longer lasting clean for environmentally concerned customers,

In an era when preserving the earth is imperative.

For a creative advertising Executive who managed several internationally successful advertising campaigns, and yet was still overlooked for a promotion, we wrote:

I am the ONLY seasoned Advertising Executive,

Who delivered 131% growth in sales to three large clients during tough economic times,

By creating innovative, viral, and award winning campaigns,

Using only a small, dedicated and loyal staff,

In an era when every advertising dollar must produce results.

Now, take the time to clearly state your ONLY value proposition.

As Marty suggest, take time to "Zag" a bit if needed, defining both what you are now, and where you need to be in the future.

As you can see, the ONLY statement answers the key value proposition and marketing points:

- **WHAT YOU DO**
- **HOW YOU DO IT**
- **WHO YOU SELL TO**
- **WHERE DO YOU SELL**
- **WHY THEY BUY**
- **WHEN (IN AN ERA)**

Sometimes called an "Elevator Pitch", the following format makes it easy:

Using the example of Harley-Davidson from Marty's "Zag",

WHAT WE DO: WE ARE THE ONLY _____
The only motorcycle manufacturer

HOW: THAT _____
that makes big, loud motorcycles

TO WHOM: TO _____
for macho guys (and macho "wannabees")

WHERE: IN _____
mostly in the United States

WHY THEY BUY: BECAUSE _____

who want to join a gang of cowboys

WHEN: IN AN ERA   _____

In an era of decreasing personal freedom

JOT DOWN YOUR ONLY STATEMENT:

WE ARE THE ONLY

_____

THAT

_____

TO

_____

IN

_____

BECAUSE

_____

IN AN ERA

_____

DONE? THEN WELL DONE!

With your ONLY statement in hand, it's time to LISTEN to your customers, your competition, and use the most powerful tools available.

Keep in mind that the ultimate goal of the Seeding (and Feeding) process is to find the most compelling area's to Lead in social selling.

As you complete the following exercises, think back to the McCourt scale and ask yourself if your customer is more likely to FIND YOU, or if they are going to be more swayed in a network where WE FIND , or if YOU FIND them.

Understanding the habits and preferences of your customer will make you a more effective marketer, will gain you access to a broader range of customers faster, and will get the most return on your investment of time and money.

Let's LISTEN....

LISTEN TO WHAT YOUR CUSTOMERS SEARCH FOR.

LIST 5 PHRASES THAT YOUR **SOCIAL** CUSTOMER IS MOST LIKELY TO GOOGLE

Think like your customer, not someone selling for a

second. What are the most basic search terms that your customer is going to start with when they go to Google, Bing, Yahoo, or any other search engine to find what they want? These search terms are called "Keywords". You're probably familiar with this process, but if not, keywords are the terms best associated with what you do and what you want the world to know about you.

For example, the Keyword Search "Discount Jeans" delivers exactly what you might expect; Ads for great prices on jeans from places like Target and Zappo's, and top organic (not paid for search results) from Old Navy and The Gap.

But, **UNLESS YOU HAVE A HUGE ADVERTISING BUDGET** like Target, The Gap, or Zappos...

THESE ARE NOT THE SOCIAL SELLING RESULTS YOU WANT!

You're looking to find where the SOCIAL customer goes to talk about jeans with other aficionados, to find key information on the latest trends, to brag about a style they love, or to see what others are passionate about.

We need to find WHERE they are social. Then we can find WHO has influence.

Using our Jeans example again, the Keyword Search "Jeans Fan" delivers a much different result than before. This time we see websites devoted exclusively to those who love jeans, Facebook pages of stylists who promote jeans as part of today's wardrobe for men and women, and bloggers who report on trends, fashion, and influences in the jean industry.

These results are the beginning of Social selling – where you **SEED (listen)** to customers at the very beginning of the selling funnel, **FEED (engage)** them to learn more and to better your business and customer service, and ultimately **LEAD (compel)** them to consider your product or service.

Now it's your turn!

Write down a list of five phrases people might use that would identify them as a potential **SOCIAL** customer of yours – **trying to USE KEYWORDS THAT DELIVER SOCIAL RESULTS**. To kick start the process, see if the following example gets your creative searching juices flowing.

Let's say you have decided to start your own line of equestrian products made of recycled materials. Your ONLY statement reads:

"We are the ONLY artisan company creating unique, beautiful equestrian products made of recycled materials, in an era (and an industry) with few innovations".

Traditional search engine keywords are:

"Equestrian Supplies"
"Equipment for A Horse"
"Horse Equipment"
"Equestrian Equipment"
"Riding Supplies"

A quick review of the powerful and useful free Google Keywords tool shows that the above list are, in fact, the highest sought after keywords for this market.

But, the search returns are not SOCIAL.

Social selling search engine keywords are:

"Horse Equipment Forum"
"Equestrian Supplies Blog"
"Horse Tack Facebook"
"Equestrian Equipment Community
"Horse Supplies Chat"

Old selling keywords deliver a wide variety of companies and individuals fighting for your dollar, while Social selling keywords invite us into a world that appreciates your eco-conscious attitude, will embrace your product, and will openly speak to its benefits, value and attributes in forums and blogs.

For example, you'll find a large and varied community of like minded horse lovers on Facebook, including pages devoted to buying and selling equipment, tack reviews, large company pages, and Mom and Pop stores.

One result is devoted to awards specifically (www. facebook.com/equestriansocialmediaawards) to recognizing those individuals that play a large role (and therefore have significant INFLUENCE) in Equestrian social media. They define their award:

"For 2013, the Equestrian Social Media Awards for the global equestrian community will nominate their favorite social media users in a variety of categories. Nominees will be subject to strict engagement criteria such as; how quickly they respond to comments, post original content, and demonstrate good online etiquette."

WOW! THAT'S YOUR GOLDMINE FOR SOCIAL SELLING!

Not all industries may give awards to recognize influencers, but in this case they have acknowledged the contribution, time and hard work it takes to be an active online citizen. And, it just so happens, for your new horse product, by LISTENING to the customer (instead of instantly trying to jump in and sell to them) we now know where they "hang out" to get advice, input and insight from others they TRUST - those in their equestrian network.

The golden rule for every businessman is this: "Put yourself in your customers place."

- Orison S Marden

THE $10 MILLION DOLLAR CUP OF COFFEE

I like to compare social selling to the story of a neighbor of ours when we lived outside of Washington DC. Over a short period, several high tech pioneers had created a boomtown overnight - led at the time by America Online. Our neighbor had done well for himself publishing award winning technical manuals, but wanted to expand the creative talents of his team into branding and design. But no matter how hard he tried, he couldn't open the doors to show off his portfolio of work because his clients came from less glamorous businesses such as manufacturing and airlines.

As was his routine, his daughter and he shared coffee and hot cocoa each morning at their local coffee shop before school. A woman in the corner was filing through papers in contemplation, when she suddenly spilled her drink on many of them. As she cleaned up with a wad of napkins, he asked the barista what she had ordered and bought her a refill.

As he handed her the drink, (she was very appreciative) and helped pick up the papers, he noticed they were all renderings of the exact logo project he had tried to pitch just a few weeks earlier.

He laughed and told her the truth "My company pitched this project not too long ago! We never got passed first base."

"What do you think?" the Executive said with obvious frustration, handing him the copies.

He studied them for few seconds, then handed them back.

"They are all wrong. We pitched you motion and strength based on a much more solid feel. These are just re-hashing the old"

As she looked to him, and then the drawings, a wide smile spread a crossed her face.

"That's exactly it! It's just the same logo. I want something new, and strong!"

Later that day Peter got his pitch in front of the full creative team, and landed a contract that ended up bringing over $10 million into his firm, as well as soon having other high tech firms lining up for his companies services.

The point? Think of old selling as the promise of a Board Room pitch where you may or may not get a chance of a contract. Social selling is the authentic act of kindness, giving information and advice (the coffee) and honest feedback (the truth about a product or service) when presented with the opportunity in a coffee house (social) setting.

NOW IT'S YOUR TURN!

WHAT ARE YOUR SOCIAL SELLING KEYWORDS?

1. _____

2. _____

3. _____

4. _____

5. _____

Think twice before you speak, because your words and influence will plant the seed of either success or failure in the mind of another.

- Napoleon Hill

The secret of my influence has always been that it remained secret.

- Salvador Dali

LISTEN TO THOSE THAT HAVE INFLUENCE.

IDENTIFY KEY INFLUENCERS IN YOUR INDUSTRY

Selling is about influence. In the past, marketers influenced our opinions by telling us benefits about their products: "A Whiter White" or "Four out of Five Doctors Recommend". Whether subtle influences, like the use of green to indicate recycled materials or eco-friendly chemicals, to the more overt "25% more!" sticker on the label, we are all influenced, and trying to influence others.

Social selling is no different. We remain influenced by the opinions, reviews and offers of others no matter if we trying to find the perfect vacation, or trying to find a cheaper replacement part of a project car.

INFLUENCE MAY NOT HAVE CHANGED...BUT THOSE THAT HAVE INFLUENCE HAS.

Today, individuals who are not employed by, do not profit from, and who are not directly connected to a product may have enormous influence over the life, death and success of that product.

This is the new era of social networking influence.

Bloggers today can sway style trends, and in turn have more influence than tried and true fashion institutions of the past like Vogue or Glamour.

As an example, on a recent episode of the NBC's TODAY show, the fashion expert, the parenting expert, and the political expert all represented blogs or online only entities.

WHO ARE YOUR INFLUENCERS?

In the earlier exercise, you used social selling keywords to find the venues that appeal to and aggregate your customer. Now you need to find the influencers within those networks.

Why? Because they have influence! Your job will be to follow them, learn from them, and ultimately to gain access to their influence by engaging and compelling them to help you.

Luckily, social influence has moved from theory to measurable science (still in its infancy, true) with metrics and tools. We'll discuss these later, so we'll focus first on understanding the influencers' roles in the social selling funnel.

Influencers provide the content of social selling, not the platform. Perhaps they have gained followers on Pinterest by always be spot-on for color predictions, or for new trends in car design. Maybe they have a blog that has thousands and thousands (maybe hundreds of thousands or millions) of devoted readers who find their simple home remedies a cost effective and preferred alternative to expensive over-the- counter medicines. Maybe they provide insight into the daily happening of young Hollywood, and by creating mass appeal they are often invited deeper into this crazy world.

Examples of influencers are as endless as the ether world itself, but the connective element is that the IN-FLUENCER has INFLUENCE over what customers' buy, whom they buy from, and when they buy. The same is true of your world. **Someone, somewhere, has influence today over your success - <u>and you need to find them.</u>**

FIND YOUR FIVE

Similar to the exercise you just completed to find your search terms and, in turn, where your customers are having conversations, lets find WHO is influencing those conversations. As a first step, lets find the **five most influential individuals** that will help you sell online in the social world.

Most likely, your social selling keywords delivered a mix of platforms where customers go to immerse themselves in the digital world you want to sell in. Let's look at the most common:

Social Networks

Influence is most sought after, and most sought out, within Social Networks.

Some companies have done great jobs developing influence in social networks. (In SEEDING STEP TWO we'll learn how to take advantage of your competition's success and gain some market share for yourself.) More importantly, however some **individuals** have significant influence within social networks and will play a key role in the success of your selling efforts.

The most obvious influencers are famous through other medias - like Ashton Kutcher or Lady Gaga who rule over nearly 13 million and 26 million twitter followers respectively. But others have gained influence by "pulling themselves up by their (digital) boot straps" to have the ear of millions as well.

For example, Veronica Belmont (@Veronica) has nearly 1.7 million Twitter followers who look for her insight on social media, and her thoughts on video gaming. It helps that she's a pretty girl that likes video games – but she is an example of the significant influence someone can build in their sphere of interest.

The same type of influencers can be found on all social networks – Facebook especially – and we'll discuss the right tools to use at the end of the Seeding chapter.

Bloggers

Outside of the confines of a Social Network, influence in pedaled in today's digital world by bloggers. Less important is the technology they use to deliver their word (Blogger, WordPress or the like), as is what they say and how it influences their audience.

Chances are that your social selling keyword exercise delivered at least one blog that your customers look to for advice or input. If not, try again. Remember,

In 2006 there were 35,000,000 bloggers.

In 2012, there were 211,000,000!

At that rate of growth, we'll see the number of blogs reach 500,000,000 in the next 5 years.

If your product, passion or project does not have some-one of influence blogging about it - **your job just got that much easier!** You'll be able to gain significant in-fluence quickly just by starting a blog yourself!

As we just pointed out, bloggers now are not only embraced by the traditional medias (TV, Radio, Adver-tising) - but they are quoted nearly as much as their main stream predecessors, and seem to be used for reviews and endorsements (just look at movie ads!) even more!

Forums

Forums are an excellent place to find influencers as well. Forums act very similar to social networks, but in most cases are more specific to a narrow focus of interest. If your social selling objectives are specific to a niche, you're more likely to find individuals interested in, and influential in your product within forums.

The healthiest competition occurs when average people win by putting above average effort.

- Colin Powell

SEED STEP TWO:
LISTEN TO YOUR COMPETITION.

WHO IS COMPETITING FOR YOUR CUSTOMER?

WHO ARE THEY RELEVANT TO?

Your competition, peers and perhaps even your co-workers are using social selling. The first response by most is worry. You ask yourself:

- Am I behind since I wasn't first?
- Does my competition already "own" the influencers?
- Am I too late to make a difference for my project?

The answer is unequivocally NO!

- NO - You're not behind!
- NO - You can easily find influencers and get to know them!
- NO - You are not too late!

In fact – you may even have the advantage! How?

In the world of social selling, you can study your competition and:

- **Learn from their strategy**

- **Appreciate what they have done right**

- **Take advantage of their missed opportunities.**

Here's how to learn from your competition.

"SHOW ME THE MONEY!"

We (perhaps of a certain age) all remember Tom Cruise's performance in the 1996 movie "Jerry Maguire" when his slick sporting agent character ends a scene with the now iconic "Show Me the Money!" mantra.

The same mantra can be used as a rallying call for finding influencers so strong that your competition has already committed hard earned money to attract.

Follow the Money Trail!

"Showing the Money" is as easy as researching advertising within social networks, search result ads, and any other social network visibility tools your competition may invest in.

Hold on to your seats – it's kind of hard to research. You:

USE YOUR FIVE SOCIAL SELLING KEYWORDS AGAIN.

That's it.

Only this time, look where your competition shows up in search returns, on ads, and in social networks.

You'll get a good sense very quickly on the priorities others have by where they place their advertising dollars.

Let's take it one step further.

Let's circle back to our 100% recycled horse tack start-up and their 5 keyword searches.

The **ORGANIC** results (those that are supplied by Google without any advertising revenue) include horse forums, horse chat rooms and horse tackle reviews.

The **PAID** results (those that are advertisements supplied by Google and paid for by companies) are plentiful, and just of few include the following:

- An Equine Supply company offering discounts and free shipping.

- A horse supplement company sponsoring a forum on understanding all there is to know on supplements.

- An Amazon.com ad for hundreds of books on horses.

- An invitation to join ongoing conversations on www. Horse.com about breeds, tackle, photos and more.

The point is this: All the results are PAID, and someone has taken the time to specifically try to grab your attention when you typed in your social selling keywords.

You are putting yourself in your customer's shoes, and seeing what your competition is paying to grab their attention with.

Lets dig deeper!

FOLLOW THE MONEY TRAIL 5 TIMES

Using your 5 social selling keyword searches, "click-thru" (click on) at least 5 advertisements in order to find where the advertiser (your competition) sells socially. Answer the following questions for each:

- How easy was it to find where they interact socially with the customer?

- Can I make it easier for my customers to interact with my company or with me?

- Where is my competition on the McCourt Scale? Do they Find Them, Find Together, or We Find?

- Can I beat the competition by using positioning myself differently on the McCourt Scale?

- Do they use the key social networks to their best advantage?
    o Are they active on Facebook?

    o Are they active on Twitter?
    o Are they active on Pinterest?
    o Are they active on LinkedIn?

If the answer is no any of these, can you prioritize that social network to out sell the competition?

Is there a pattern? Does your competition use Facebook quite a bit, but ignore twitter? Do they favor Twitter, but just a few use Pinterest? If so, focus on the social network that represents the most initial opportunity.

Do your competitors offer an easy to access "portal" to social activities about our area of interest? If not, you can be that person.
Here's an easy format for this exercise.

FINDING YOUR COMPETITIVE ADVANTAGE

1. My competitor's ad from the keyword search
_____ shows they are selling on
_____ social network but not
_____.

2. My competitor's ad from the keyword search
_____ shows they are selling on
_____ social network but not
_____.

3. My competitor's ad from the keyword search
_____ shows they are selling on
_____ social network but not
_____.

4. My competitor's ad from the keyword search
_____ shows they are selling on
_____ social network but not
_____.

5. My competitor's ad from the keyword search
_____ shows they are selling on
_____ social network but not
_____.

Based on these results, I should focus on the _____ social network first for my social selling efforts.

We'll spend more time working with the competition in our FEED exercises as well, but remember that your competition has already supplied you with a path to influential customers, has already told you what they believe are key social selling platforms, and where they have decided to spend their dollars.

You're job is to simply decide where you can create an advantage, to find networks that could yield better results and have more opportunity, and where you can beat them at their own game!

so, SEED = LISTEN

LISTEN TO YOUR CUSTOMER.

LISTEN TO YOUR COMPETITION.

KNOW YOUR TARGET AUDIENCE.

CREATE YOUR ONLY STATEMENT.

USE YOUR ONLY STATEMENT TO CREATE YOUR 5 SO-CIAL SELLING KEYWORD STATEMENTS.

YOUR KEYWORD STATEMENTS DEFINE YOUR SOCIAL SELLING SPACE.

FIND THE TOP INFLUENCERS IN YOUR SOCIAL SELLING NETWORKS.

LET YOUR COMPETITION GUIDE YOUR SOCIAL SELL-ING EFFORTS.

It is not your customer's job to remember you.

- Patricia Fripp

SEED STEP THREE:
TODAY'S TOOLS

HERES THE BEST TOOLS TO SEED TODAY.

New tools constantly become available, so make sure you check at

www.orfail.com/seedtools

for updates.

BUT FIRST – OUR "RULES ON TOOLS"

We are cheap. And we believe that in today's competitive online environment, software and online tool providers have to offer the best, for the least cost. Therefore, you'll find…

WE DO NOT RECOMMEND ANY SOFTWARE THAT DOES NOT PROVIDE A FREE TRIAL PERIOD, and

WE PREFER FREE TOOLS WHENEVER POSSIBLE.

With that said, as of this edition, the tools we recommend for the SEED process are:

ONLY STATEMENT TOOLS

LET HARVARD HELP

Many times we create our only statements with the help of

www.alumni.hbs.edu/careers/pitch/

The Harvard Business School has created an easy to use, insightful online tool to help define your ONLY statement. In this case, they use the "Elevator Pitch" metaphor:

"You have one minute (in an elevator) to explain your-self, your business, your goals, and your passions…to an audience that knows none of these."

Obviously you could use your ONLY statement as your elevator pitch! So we suggest going through Harvard's wonderful program. It's open to anyone, and free.

STEAL THIS IDEA

It's obvious we are fans of MARTY NEUMEIER and Liquid Agency – and they are kind enough to provide free access to brand concept and thinking tools that will help you "zag", and inspire your ONLY statement. Visit:

http://www.liquidagency.com/blog/

Aptly named "STEAL THIS IDEA", you'll find the tools, exercises, insight and updates that are wonderful.

SOCIAL SELLING KEYWORD TOOLS

GOOGLE KEYWORD TOOL

Let Google guide the way. Google is kind enough (hey – it benefits them, so not really that magnanimous) to give anyone free access to their powerful keyword tool. Visit:

https://adwords.google.com/o/KeywordTool

It looks like this:

BEWARE: THE GOOGLE ADWORD KEYWORD TOOL IS **FREE**. IF THERE IS A FEE FOR THE TOOL, THEN YOU PROBABLY FOUND A SNEAKY SITE PRETENDING TO BE ASSOCIATED WITH GOOGLE.

With the Google Keyword Tool you can type in your own entries and see the popularity of your keywords. The process will help you define social selling vs. selling keywords.

We also suggest using their website tool that allows you to enter a website address (url) of a site you think is similar, a competitor, or a peer. Google will return their keywords!

You'll also find plenty of videos, training materials and expert advice on getting the most out of the Google Keyword Tool.

Two more Google Tools are worth mentioning as well.

GOOGLE OFFERS INSIGHTS

Still in it's infancy, Google has introduced a search "insight" tool at:

www.google.com/insights/search/

By allowing you to narrow down statistics and information on a particular search term (in this case your 5 social selling keywords!) to a specific category, the insight search tool helps you find the seasonality of terms, find related terms and their popularity, and find other terms that are trending up from customers.

GOOGLE TRENDS

In unison with Insights, Google offers additional information on customer search habits with:

www.google.com/trends/

We use Trends as a way to compare the interest in different topics and different search terms. Trends is particularly helpful if you are trying to find regional and international trends for a particular subject.

Other tools we use include several subscription options with free trials.

LOOK TO THE BOOK (SEOBOOK)

Seobook.com offers a free account with access to quite a few good search keywords tools. Go to:

www.seobook.com

Of course they are going to try to sell you a paid for subscription that offer more detailed and in depth tools, as well as expert help. But dig around and see if you like their services before taking that leap.

TRACK THOSE WORDS

WordTracker has been a staple of search tools for many years at:

www.wordtracker.com

They have recently reduced their free trial to a week, so use your time wisely! WordTracker provides several strategy tools and is more powerful than most finding true social selling keywords.

FINDING INFLUENCER TOOLS

BE A TECHNORATI

The art and science of finding influencers has merged together in the past few years, and new tools and options are being introduced every day. Many are very, very sophisticated (Radian6 for example) and come with a big price tag.

If your project or business can afford these types, by all means use them. For the beginner (and price conscience) we like:

www.technorati.com

as a good place to start your influencer search. Technorati offers a broad range of blogs and forums that are currently discussing your search term(s).

GOOGLES GOT BLOG

Google provides a powerful blog search tool to identify influencers, at:

www.google.com/blogsearch

Our suggestion would be to find a range of influencer options you want to investigate (using these and other tools), and then quantify their influence using several key metrics.

MEASURING INFLUENCE WITH ALEXA

Similar to Google Analytics, the Alexa toolbar and dashboard (free tools) can be found at:

www.alexa.com

Some controversy surrounds the true value and measurement of several of the metrics, but we agree with most experts that this Amazon.com provided service has a broad enough base of data input (from users with the toolbar downloaded) to give users a good sense of a sites web traffic and ranking.

In LEAD, we'll dive into metrics in more detail, and suggest more powerful tools specifically designed to measure social influence, but for the exercise of finding influencers, Alexa can provide metric information on:

Alexa Traffic Rank: A ranking on the popularity of a site as indexed by Alexa.

Traffic Rank in USA: A ranking on the popularity of a site in the USA – using data from sources outside of Alexa.

Reviews: Comments from other Alexa users on a site.

Sites Linking In: The number of other websites that link TO the site you are looking at. The higher the links, the more search engines believe in the websites power and use.

Search Analytics: A useful review of search terms and related metrics that drive traffic to this site. USE THIS TOOL TO SEE WHAT DRIVES CUSTOMERS TO YOUR COMPETITION!

Wayback Machine: Alexa records historical "snapshots" of websites in the past. If you want to see a visual record of a website, this is a great tool to do so.

Related Links: Alexa provides a list of sites that are "related" to the website you are reviewing – usually in the form of competitors sites that are usually returned in a search. For example, when you search for "The Gap", "Old Navy" is a related link, as well as other subsidiaries the Gap owns.

Fast: Alexa calculates the average time it takes to load a site into a browser for viewing. Slow sites usually turn away customers faster than sites with acceptable load times.

FEED =
KNOW WHERE TO ENGAGE

PART FOUR

HOW TO FEED:
YOUR STEP-BY-STEP GUIDE

Congratulations are in order! You have completed the hardest part of the SEED, FEED, and LEAD process by doing your seeding exercises. Now the fun begins! We are closer than ever to social selling because we now Feed, or Engage, with the customer. Again, follow our **3 easy feeding steps:**

STEP ONE:
KNOW WHERE TO ENGAGE

STEP TWO:
RULES OF ENGAGEMENT

STEP THREE:
ENGAGE WITH THE RIGHT TOOLS

Dream more than others think practical... Expect more than others think possible.

- Howard Schultz

FEED STEP ONE:
KNOW WHERE TO ENGAGE

WHERE IS YOUR TARGET AUDIENCE?

IT'S YOUR TIME TO INFLUENCE!

In the SEEDING steps, we spent time defining your ONLY statement, and applying what makes up your project, company – or you! – special. We also began the discovery process of identifying individuals who have influence in your social arena.

In the FEEDING steps, we continue our work with INFLUENCE – by deciding WHERE to ENGAGE to deliver your best social selling results. We'll revisit the McCourt Scale to pinpoint the social networks that will lead your way, and we'll speak to the simple, easy to understand rules of engagement that will deliver customers right to your door, and keep them coming back.

It's time to engage and influence your customers!

BACK TO THE FUTURE – THE MCCOURT SCALE.

You probably have a better understanding of your customer's online preferences already.

- Are they communicative and like forums where there is plenty of interaction?

- Perhaps they are a bit more voyeuristic; reading blogs but rarely commenting.

- Are they visually driven? Preferring to be inspired by social networks that share pictures and videos?

- Or are they networking animals? Constantly connecting and building relationships in order to grow their own influence?

Under any of these circumstances, it's time to decide which social selling area your customer prefers.

Circle back to the McCourt scale, this time keeping in mind your **ONLY** statement, your **SOCIAL SELLING** keywords, and where you found your **KEY INFLUENCERS**.

Ask yourself the key **McCourt Influence** questions:

YOU FIND IT: Are your customers most likely to dig around the digital world to discover information, feedback, reviews and deals on your products and services?

WE FIND IT: Do your customers seek to share their everyday life experiences, to communicate, and to find information they trust from a network for purchasing input?

IT FINDS YOU: Does your customer prefer the entire purpose of the social experience to be devoted to selling? Does your customer like to be "told" of a deal through a daily deal site, or like to be presented with an array of new deals on your products and services?

Take time to really study the McCourt Scale, and the spectrum of social selling options it represents. You may find that your customer DOES NOT have a preference, and that good examples of social selling efforts and influence abound in all areas. Or you may find a precise and distinct area where your customers network.

YOUR CUSTOMERS CHOICE

By keeping your customer in mind, putting yourself in their shoes, and committing to connect with them on an authentic level (not solely on a commercial level) – you'll be rewarded with clear choices and direction that represents your customer's choice.

As humans however, we may have a preconceived notion of where to network and in turn, where to sell.

You need to throw out these notions, and look at your social selling plan from a fresh point of view.

For example...

Love Facebook? Have you been an active Facebook user for years, staying in contact with friends and family, Liking sites and supporting causes that interest you? **But does your customer?**

Love Twitter? Have you broadcast witty insights and built a loyal following of others who are impressed with your intellect and humor? **But does your customer care?**

Love Pinterest? Do you have a keen eye for the latest trends presented in an appealing, visual format like Pinterest? Are you a "curator" of what's new and like to let others know of your insight? **But does your customer like the same?**

The point is simple: Your customer has a choice. That choice is which social network they spend their networking time, and most likely it is the network that gives them informative content quickly, in a format they enjoy. In a moment we'll use the McCourt Scale to help in that process. But before we do, there is one other choice to make. Yours.

YOUR CHOICE

You have to prioritize the social networks that most

interest your customers, and where your most sup-
portive and influential customers interact.

You can, however, prioritize social selling in a forum or
network that you are familiar with, and proficient at.
If you're a Whiz at Flickr, then make one of your Top 3
Flickr. If you live on Google +, then make one of your
Top 3 Google +.

By optimizing the hard work you have already put into
your social networking efforts, you can offset some of
the ramp-up time you will need for other networks by
adding a "known commodity" into the mix!

"Seek, Learn, Grow...Or Fail" ™

PRIORITIZE YOUR TOP 3

Here's the McCourt Scale as we first reviewed it.

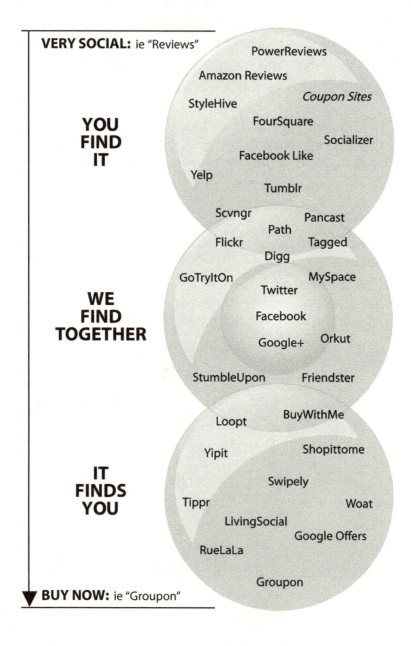

VERY SOCIAL: ie "Reviews"

PowerReviews

Amazon Reviews

StyleHive · *Coupon Sites*

YOU FIND IT

FourSquare

Socializer

Facebook Like

Yelp

Tumblr

Scvngr · Pancast

Path

Flickr · Tagged

Digg

GoTryItOn · MySpace

Twitter

WE FIND TOGETHER

Facebook

Google+ · Orkut

StumbleUpon · Friendster

Loopt · BuyWithMe

Yipit · Shopittome

IT FINDS YOU

Swipely

Tippr · Woat

LivingSocial

Google Offers

RueLaLa

Groupon

BUY NOW: ie "Groupon"

Now, lets use the McCourt Scale again to commit to your Top 3 networks that you will SEED, FEED and LEAD!

VERY SOCIAL: ie "Reviews"

PowerReviews

Amazon Reviews

Top 3 "You Find It" Sites:

StyleHive

Coupon Sites

FourSquare

Socializer

Facebook Like

Yelp

Tumblr

_____

_____

_____

Scvngr

Pancast

Path

Flickr

Tagged

Digg

Top 3 "We Find It" Sites:

GoTryItOn

MySpace

Twitter

Facebook

_____

_____

_____

Google+

Orkut

StumbleUpon

Friendster

BuyWithMe

Loopt

Top 3 "It Finds You" Sites:

Yipit

Shopittome

Swipely

_____

_____

_____

Tippr

Woat

LivingSocial

Google Offers

RueLaLa

▼ **BUY NOW:** ie "Groupon"

Groupon

Take a look at your Top 3. If your customer likes each category of social network site (YOU, WE and IT FIND) then you'll have 9 to choose from.

Now, to narrow your efforts to find your Top 3, take some time to review each site you've listed and choose based on the following criteria:

- Are you comfortable with it?
- Is the site expanding (number of new users is growing)?
- Do you have multiple influential users in the site?
- Does the site have easy to access tools and good ways engage potential customers?
- Is it "Your Choice"? Do you already have expertise with it?

The sites that you answer YES to these criteria are the best sites for your Top 3!

MY TOP 3 SOCIAL SELLING SITES:

1. _____

2. _____

3. _____

NOW THE FUN BEGINS! TIME TO SIGN ON THE (DIGITAL) BOTTOM LINE.

Congratulations! You have your Top 3!

Now it's time to begin the "real work" of developing your digital presence, reaching out to customers and influencers, and creating metrics that help gauge the success of your social selling efforts!

In virtually all cases, signing up for each network will be straightforward. Almost all are free. Many prefer that you use an existing peer network (Facebook being the most popular) to sign up.

Our suggestion is to NOT use a peer network initially to set up your Top 3. Why? Because, as you begin your social selling efforts, you probably don't want everyone to track all your steps and actions. Yet.

WE CAN HELP

Each network does have it's own character, and we have learned "tricks of the trade" and short cuts that may help your process.

Go to

www.orfail.com/feedsteps

and **download** all the feeding steps in an easy to use document format, as well as get insight on the Feed process.

Yesterday's home runs don't win today's games.

- Babe Ruth

FEED STEP TWO:
RULES OF ENGAGEMENT

YOU KNOW WHERE, BUT DO YOU KNOW HOW TO ENGAGE?

THE ART OF BEING HUMAN

Feeding social networks in order to create more interest in (and sales of) your product runs almost counter-intuitive to the sales practices of yesteryear. And by "yesteryear" we mean sales practices of less than a decade ago.

Today, customers and consumers want access to information about each and every purchase. They want reviews untainted by the manufacturers claims, and they want honest input from others who have bought before them, or are considering as well.

Look at the process of social selling today, compared to selling in the past, with this analogy.

You've decided to buy a car, and you have narrowed down your wish list to two models. In the past, you would take time out of your busy life to go down to the dealership of each brand. You're greeted by a salesperson who compliments your choice, rattles off statistics about the car, and tries to move you quickly inside the showroom to make a deal.

Since you're a smart buyer, your resist his pressure tactics and you and your family jump inside, enjoy the new car smell, and take a test drive. You haggle with the salesperson until you found a price you're comfortable with.

You would do this for each car choice, then based on your observations, your feel for the car, the test ride, the roominess and probably even the color and the look of the wheels – you would decide on your new car.

Today, with social selling, it's more like taking your family – as well as a bus full of other prepared individuals who are ready for any question you may have with vast statistics, superior negotiation skills, thousands of reviews, and experience with the same car.

Can you imagine how intimidating it would be to the salesperson if you showed up on Saturday with an RV of friends, experts and a handful of previous customers to buy your car?

Chances are you would have a lot more confidence negotiating for a great deal if you had 6 other customers talk about their experience first, then reviewed the price of the same car at a dealer just down the road, then took a few minutes to speak to the car's reviews, then (just for fun) reviewed the same information for the other car you are considering.

That's the power of Social Selling!

And since, in this example, <u>you're the salesperson</u>, you could very well be intimidated. But don't be! Because if you harness the power of social selling, if you understand your role and how to engage, you'll soon be the preferred choice for each and every one of your customers.

How? You just need to be **GREAT!**

TO TRULY BE ENGAGING, YOU JUST NEED TO BE G.R.E.A.T!

Social selling is part science, part art. Part objective, part subjective. The objective aspects can easily be measured (and we'll discuss these metrics in a bit), while the subjective part is practically immeasurable.

And yet it's the most important.

This subjective aspect of social selling, many times called your "voice", is something you will develop and hone over time. You'll get into a rhythm of knowing what engages online, and what is not as successful.

What we found, however, is that to have a great "voice", you must be **G.R.E.A.T:**

- **GENUINE**
- **RELATABLE**
- **ENTERTAINING**
- **AMAZING**
- **TRUSTWORTHY**

GENUINE
Honest. Authentic. Genuine.

Being genuine is the cornerstone of both engaging, and social selling. Throw away the tricks of the trade you've used in the past to close deals, and relate to your customer from a basis of honesty.

Today, no matter where they are, your customer is your neighbor. By being honest, being your true self, and being genuine with every action you take, you'll engage on a much deeper level with every customer.

RELATABLE
Approachable. Obtainable. Relatable.

Connect with customers on their own level. Sure, you may be a world expert on a product, on yourself, or on your opinions, but you'll never truly engage and build a strong foundation for social selling unless you are approachable.

Today, you are a teacher as much as you are a salesperson. By making yourself relatable – even if it means showing weakness by not knowing an answers, or having an issue you need to address on a product – you'll truly gain support and trust from your influencers and customers.

ENTERTAINING
Clever. Fascinating. Entertaining.

Very few people can be funny "on command". It's hard to come up with witty comments and pithy content all the time. But to be engaging, you have to approach your social interaction with a flair for the whimsy.

Today, you're an entertainer as much as you are a salesperson. So have fun with your content. Let your "inner funny-bone" come out through your on-line voice. Take time to think about your interaction, and challenge yourself to make it more interesting. Is there a "sub-story" (a related aspect to your subject that adds interest) that both helps support your efforts, as well as gives an entertaining spin on it. If there is, then use it!

Bottom-line – **have fun!**

AMAZING
Impressive. Astonishing. Amazing.

A simple way to be amazing at social selling is to do things others would not. It's not in our nature to open ourselves up to our customers, our peers and our competition. But in the world of social selling, true engagement is being transparent.

Today, when you are genuine, relatable, and entertaining – you'll also be amazing! Being impressive will be a "by-product" of all your other G.R.E.A.T efforts. But push yourself to go a step further. Always be thinking of ways to differentiate yourself from your competitors. Put yourself in your customer's shoes and figure out what would compel them to choose you. Review what your competitors do that amazes you and improve on it!

Always be on the search for related or unrelated promotions, advertising, blog and forum conversations, and any other social interaction that you can put to your own use.

We keep a folder on our shared desktop and challenge everyone on our team to put 10 new ideas each week into it. Years later, we have a library of THOUSANDS of great ideas!

TRUSTWORTHY
Forthright. Reliable. Trustworthy.

Successful social selling requires individuals to do what they say they will do. Never promise what you cannot deliver. Never over-sell the benefits and features of your product, unless it truly provides them. Never over-sell your skills and qualifications.

Today, trustworthy companies have more social value than their competitors. By being honest, reliable and delivering on your promises, you'll soon receive great reviews that people trust, and you'll engage your customers confidence, knowing that you can follow thru on your word.

Remember, successful social selling means you have to **FEED** content, information and conversations in order to **ENGAGE** your customers.

The best way to **ENGAGE** is to be **G.R.E.A.T!**

You'll be fantastic at social selling if you make it your mission to be:

- **GENUINE**
- **RELATABLE**
- **ENTERTAINING**
- **AMAZING**
- **TRUSTWORTHY**

In fact, you'll be so successful that editors, bloggers and social networks will want you to be a **PUBLISHER!** We'll discuss this as part of the LEADING process. But first, social selling means you are an editor as well.

Here's why...

"

The great accomplishments of man have resulted from the transmission of ideas of enthusiasm.

- Thomas J. Watson

ON YOUR MARK, GET SET, EDIT!

Our new world of selling centers around the new world of publishing. Far from the traditional sense of publishing, every post we make, every article we submit, every Facebook update, every Tweet, (basically every time we communicate online) is part of the new publishing world. And good communication is appreciated, sought after, and rewarded.

The reward is viral, massive, and wide-spread use of the content you provide. GREAT content, however, takes time, concentration and effort to create.

It's worth taking a bit of time here to review the fundamentals of the unique, useful, and engaging content you're about ready to create.

Let's take a look.

ENGAGING CONTENT IS USEFUL AND UNIQUE

As we learned earlier, engaging content is like a great coffeehouse conversation. It's casual, entertaining, and gets your creative juices flowing. In other words, content has VALUE when it's:

USEFUL	UNIQUE
EDUCATIONAL	CREATIVE
INFORMATIVE	ORIGINAL
ENTERTAINING	CLEVER
BENEFICIAL	EXCLUSIVE
RELEVANT	PERSONAL

USEFUL CONTENT HAS VALUE

Your social selling content (the content that drives customers to your site, and compels them to purchase) has to add value somehow.

For example, this means you have to provide information that keeps the customer up to date, giving them the latest insight into what is happening to you, your product, and your industry.

Also, useful content has to be beneficial, and solve a specific need for them. Always put yourself in the customer's shoes, and think about how you can solve the most common problems they encounter.

Relevancy is also a key part of great content, authentically reaching out to provide useful, educational conversations that interest, entertain, and provide knowledge.

UNIQUE CONTENT HAS VALUE

At the same time, your social selling efforts will be more valuable when it is unique. Why? Because very few content providers – whether it's comments, bloggers, or your competitors – take the time to make their content creative and clever.

Much of today's content is stale, re-hashed, and impersonal.

By concentrating on your own voice, insuring you are unique and original, you'll create a social selling platform that others gravitate towards.

We'll spend the last step – where you **LEAD** – understanding more about how to be unique and **COMPEL** customers to purchase from you. But for now…

AS CAPT. KIRK SAYS – **"ENGAGE!"**

Engage! Ahead warp factor 2! You have your orders. Now Go!

You have listened to your customer, and you have listened to your competition in order to know who and where to provide GREAT ENGAGEMENT.

Your content will be USEFUL and UNIQUE, and will add significant value to your customer's lives and help in their decision process.

You know WHERE to ENGAGE, WHO YOUR ENGAGING WITH, and by adding Genuine, Relatable, Entertaining, Amazing and Trustworthy content you're sure to succeed!

SO, FEED = **ENGAGE**

KNOW WHERE TO ENGAGE YOUR CUSTOMER.

FOLLOW THE RULES OF ENGAGEMENT.

USE THE MCCROURT SCALE AGAIN TO FIND YOUR TOP 3 PLACES TO ENGAGE YOUR TARGET AUDIENCE.

BE MINDFUL OF YOUR CUSTOMERS CHOICE, AND RESPECT YOUR OWN CHOICE.

BE HUMAN AND CREATE G.R.E.A.T. ENGAGEMENT BY BEING GENUINE, RELATABLE, ENTERTAINING, AMAZING, AND TRUSTWORTHY.

G.R.E.A.T CONTENT THAT IS USEFUL AND UNIQUE WILL HAVE SIGNIFICANT VALUE – AND COMPEL YOUR CUSTOMERS TO PURCHASE!

"

If I have accomplished anything in life, it is because I have been willing to work hard.

- *C. J. Walker*

FEED STEP THREE:
ENGAGE WITH THE RIGHT TOOLS

HERE'S THE BEST TOOLS TO FEED TODAY.

As we said before, new tools constantly become available, so make sure you check at

www.orfail.com/feedtools

for updates.

WHERE TO ENGAGE TOOLS

DO YOU HAVE KLOUT?

Klout provides an easy to use, free tool to find influencers, and rank your own influence in social media networks.

www.klout.com

Klout tools scour the largest social networks for data, and measures influence to show users how they impact the people connected to them.

Thousands of categories and topics are covered, and each venue (whether its an individual like yourself, a blog, a forum, or other network) receives a "Klout Score", narrowing down the most influential venues that can help you sell socially.

IF NOT KLOUT, MAYBE SOME KRED(IBILITY)

Kred is another very good tool to find where to engage your customer. It's both a bit more complicated than other tools, but more sophisticated and powerful as well.

www.kred.com

Kred provides a comprehensive A-Z list of communities (things like wine tasting, acting, fantasy football and hundreds of others), as well as good tools to find your own niche.

Kred does a nice job pinpointing influencers, and gives you a good visual representation of location (where you're influencers are) and what tools they use to communicate.

LEARN ABOUT YOUR PEERINDEX

Peerindex is similar to Klout, providing a set of social media analytic tools for free. They have also integrated a reward program (PeerPerks) that create discounts and value as you become a more influential user, and as you work more in social networks.

www.peerindex.com

Peerindex measures a venues influence by providing statistics on Activity, Authority, and Audience. Activity is straightforward – how often you engage in social activities. Authority measures how relevant your activity has been in the community, and indicates when other like, comment and/or engage with your activity.

Audience measures reach relative to the rest of the population, giving you a scale of how deep, and important your engagement has been.

PEEKYOU GIVES YOU A PEEK-A-BOO

Peekyou's format is a bit more "tabloid" looking – but don't underestimate it's power to find where your influential customers, critiques and content providers are.

www.peekyou.com

It's hard not to get addicted to the blend of "name brand" influencers (usually celebrities, politicians, and others who have already achieved some sort of following from their fame), as well as others who have truly created a name for themselves in their venue.

Peekyou also provides a 1 – 10 scale score of influence (the Peekscore), and does a nice job detailing influence a crossed a very wide variety of social networks.

G.R.E.A.T CONTENT TOOLS

GREAT CONTENT IDEAS FOR INSPIRATION

It's not too hard to be inspired to create GREAT content if you spend just a few minutes perusing the web. Sometimes, however, you'll find yourself seemingly out of good content ideas. To get started, you may find it useful to take a look at:

SLIDESHARE.NET
Slideshare allows users to post, review and even download slide presentations on thousands of topics. It's an excellent source of inspiration and ideas.

LISTVERSE.COM
Listverse is devoted to the art of the "Top 10" list. Nearly 3 million users enjoy thousands of lists that intrigue, educate and entertain.

BUZZFEED.COM
Using a "tabloid" format, Buzzfeed features social news on trending topics and viral topics.

VOICES.YAHOO.COM
Yahoo provides, in a newly revamped format and

platform, a great place to find content of similar interest. We particularly like the easy to use layout, and the rich library of user provided videos.

HUBPAGES.COM

Hubpages is a hip, modern take on content development and distribution. With over 50 million monthly users, it's a good site to help find your audience.

SQUIDOO.COM

Squidoo is the brainchild of social and online marketing guru Seth Godin, whose numerous books we highly recommend. You'll find a wide variety of topics presented in a visual format (much in the same way Pinterest works).

HUBSPOT.COM

Clearly Hubspot is a profit driven site, but we appreciate the free access to great content via their blogs, and their constant creation and large library of whitepapers, surveys and infographics.

CONTENTLY.COM

Contently is a more robust publishing and journalistic platform with a free version. It allows for significant access to some great content, but is a little more cumbersome to set up and use than others. As your content needs get more robust, keep Contently on your long-term list.

SUITE101.COM

Suite101 is a clean, fun, intuitive format that collects great content from users in the form of "channels" devoted to a particular subject. It's addicting! You'll find you can loose track of time pretty quickly – but ultimately you'll find great inspiration for your content.

"Seek, Learn, Grow...Or Fail" ™

Winston, if I were your wife, I would put poison in your coffee.

- Lady Nancy Astor

Nancy, if I were your husband, I would drink it.

- Winston Churchill

LEAD =
KNOW HOW
TO COMPEL

PART FIVE

HOW TO LEAD:
YOUR STEP-BY-STEP GUIDE

To LEAD, you'll get your creative side ready to build GREAT STORIES that COMPEL your customer to take action! We'll also create compelling promotions (not gimmicks) that fulfill their wants and needs. Follow our **3 easy leading steps:**

STEP ONE:
TELL COMPELLING STORIES

STEP TWO:
OFFER COMPELLING PROMOTIONS

STEP THREE:
COMPEL WITH THE RIGHT TOOLS

You are what you repeatedly do. Excellence is not an event - it is a habit.

- Aristotle

LEAD STEP ONE:
TELL COMPELLING STORIES

LEAD YOUR TARGET AUDIENCE TO BUY!

MAKE YOUR INFLUENCE COMPELLING!

Everything comes together in the last step of SEED, FEED, and LEAD. You have your ONLY statement, have listened to your customer, and know (and how!) to engage them. You're ready to create G.R.E.A.T content with your authentic voice to gain INFLUENCE from your social selling efforts.

Now it's time to make that INFLUENCE COMPELLING!

IT'S TIME TO LEAD!

The good news is LEADING allows your creative nature to join your business acumen. You'll learn how to create GREAT STORIES in order to communicate the VALUE of your brand to your influencers, your customers, your peers (and your competitors!)

STORIES ARE WHO WE ARE (ALL OF US)

Before we start, let's clear up a potential misconception as we create your story.

Telling a story is not lying.

Bestselling author and influential blogger Seth Godin, in his book *"All Marketers Tell Stories,"* says *"Stories make it easier to understand the world. Stories are the way we know how to spread an idea. Marketers didn't invent storytelling. They just perfected it."*

Great social sellers, (and in fact all great marketing) is based on a great story that has a likable hero who encounters an obstacle or roadblock, only to overcome it against all odds and emerge transformed.

Whether it's the first Star Wars movie, or the incredibly successful *"You're gonna love the way you look, you have my word on it"* advertising slogan used for nearly 20 years by George Zimmer, founder of Mens Warehouse clothing stores.

All good marketing is based on great stories.

In fact, you can make a solid case that all aspects of our culture, our identities and our beliefs (our own individual reality) are based on stories we all know, believe, and tell others.

All cultures, since the creation of human language, and all cultures that will exist well beyond us, have been built on stories, and will continue to include stories.

More than ever, stories are becoming a more important aspect of who we are, and what we sell.

Why are stories so important in todays age of instant

access to facts, data and information? Simple.

Our left brains are running out of stuff to do.

As we run (not walk) towards our "knowledge worker" economy, technology is playing a larger role in left brain work.

In humans, the left brain controls the logical, analytical and objective aspects of our thought process. The right brain has the creative, thoughtful and subjective responsibilities. Technology, at its very core, has been designed to take over much of the left brained tasks, while creative (right brained) stuff still falls to us humans.

In his breakthrough book about this future, *"A Whole New Mind"*, Daniel Pink says:

"L-Directed (left brain controlled) aptitudes—the sorts of things measured by the SAT and deployed by CPAs— are still necessary. But they're no longer sufficient. Instead, the R-Directed (Right brain controlled) aptitudes so often disdained and dismissed—artistry, empathy, taking the long view, pursuing the transcendent—will increasingly determine who soars and who stumbles."

So get your writers cap on! Stories, narratives, and scripts are the road from the past, the way of the future, and a key part of social selling!

Luckily, stories within social selling and social networks can be created by following simple steps to be compelling, engaging and powerful. We'll learn how to utilize a proven foundation of great story telling and apply it to communicating your brand, your project, or you!

Ready to LEAD? Lets go!

CREATE A COMPELLING STORY: YOURS

You have a compelling story. Maybe you're tasked with starting a new web store. Maybe you're taking a traditional brand and trying to reenergize it. Maybe you need more clients, customers, followers, resellers, or students.

Whatever your needs, your story is already there, ready to be written.

We're going to write one of the most compelling stories ever. **Yours!**

ELEMENTS OF GREAT STORIES

Let's say you got the following email.

"Hey There,

My name is Tim, and I'm a friend of Dave's. I happened to be at his party on Friday and he told me about what has happened to you. I have to admit it's pretty compelling, and I'm in charge of new story development for EntertainCo here in Hollywood. I think there would be interest in getting it on paper for some of the movie execs here. Can we talk? Thanks – Tim"

Did something come right to mind when you read that? Did "…what happened to you" suddenly stir up a new or old memory? Did you see, in a flash, your story on the Big Screen?

Well then, that's your story!

But, maybe what flashed in your head is personal – and not what you need for your social selling. Then re-read Tim's email within the context of what Tim needs for a script you can sell the Hollywood studio movie execs your movie.

Movies are our modern cultures cleanest and quickest way to tell stories. All over the world, everyday, hundreds of new movies are released. 95% of them follow the same format, even though the stories they tell may be wildly different. The format is:

- **Relatable and Likable Hero**
- **Encounters Roadblocks**
- **But Emerges Transformed**

Lets look at some classic movie script examples using this format.

Horror Story

Five attractive college kids on summer break decide to visit a distant uncles cabin deep in the woods of Maine, only to find out it's haunted by murders past.

In three acts of selfless heroism to save the others, two kids survive to warn others.

- **Relatable Hero's: Five college kids**
- **Roadblocks: Haunted cabin**
- **Emerge: Transformed by selfless acts of others**

Action Story
A CIA agent and his wife, on vacation celebrating his retirement, witness the abduction of a prominent businessman by a known terrorist group. Realizing the group intends on executing the man at sundown, they devise a brilliant and risky plan to save him.

- **Relatable Hero's: CIA agent and wife**
- **Roadblocks: Terrorist group**
- **Emerge: Triumphant after risking all to save the businessman**

Love Story
After 30 years of marriage, and a bitter divorce, a couple unwittingly finds themselves on their second marriage honeymoons in a beautiful hotel in Paris – where they had dreamed about honeymooning before. Circumstances throw them together in different parts of the city, and they realize their new partners are not who they thought they were, and that their own love is still stronger than ever.

- **Relatable Hero's: The couple**
- **Roadblocks: Divorce and second marriages**
- **Emerge: More in love than ever**

Very different stories for sure, but see how they all have the elements of classic story structure? They all have hero's who encounter trouble, figure out a way to overcome, and emerges transformed.

Let's write your movie!

BACK TO YOUR ONLY STATEMENT

Go back and review your **ONLY** statement.

(If you didn't take the time to write it before, shame on you! Do it now! It's important for your Movie).

One of the easiest ways to create your social media and branding story is to wrap it around the conviction and position you have already defined in your ONLY statement.

Let's look at the ONLY statement example from earlier:

We are the ONLY children's outdoor apparel retailer,

Who sells high quality, traditional inspired styles,

In neighborhood locations,

To parents who want their kids to live playful, balanced lives,

In an era when kids grow up too fast.

Now take a moment to see the story inherent in this ONLY statement. It has all the elements needed:

- **Relatable Hero's: Children unable to play outdoors**
- **Roadblock: Growing up in the technological era**
- **Emerge: Transformed into balanced, playful kids ready to face the world**

What would the movie be?

Family Movie
When an eccentric Aunt moves into the Smith family household, she is mortified by the technological infatuation of her sister's kids. Growing up in the wilds of Montana, she unsuccessfully tries to interest the kids in the outdoors. But when her sister and brother in-law leave for a business trip, she forces her nieces and nephew to live in their backyard the entire time. The parents return to kids full of imagination and a new attitude on life.

What great social selling this ONLY statement and STORY will be! The children and the Aunt will fascinate people. What did they cook outdoors? How did they sleep? What did they do without the Internet and video games?

We can use this same exercise for your STORY. Here's how:

- **Review your ONLY statement**

- **Surround your Story around your ONLY statement**
- **Create your own Movie Script**
- **Make sure you create G.R.E.A.T stories**

MAKE YOUR STORY YOUR MOVIE: IT'S AS EASY AS 1 – 2 – 3

Movies are programmatic. Not every single movie, but certainly all of the blockbuster hits since the release of the first "talkie" follow classic storytelling cadence.

Syd Field, story guru and author of *"Screenplay: The Foundations of Screenwriting,"* has clearly laid out the ideal story paradigm in his definition of stories (movies in this case) having three distinct parts.

Act 1 (The Setup) – Establish the stories hero's and what the roadblock to overcome is going to be.

Act 2 (The Conflict) – The Hero's attempt to resolve the roadblock, only to be thwarted. New skills and solutions are necessary to attempt again.

Act 3 (The Resolution) – The Hero's emerges transformed, and have a new sense of who they really are.

Or, going back to our movie script examples:

Act 1 – Relatable and Likable Hero
Act 2 - Encounters Roadblocks
Act 3 - But Emerges Transformed

Before we start using this paradigm for our own purposes (to write your story), think of the movies you may have in your DVD collection that follow this classic pattern. As you look the titles, take a second to figure out the Hero's, the Roadblocks, and how they Emerge Transformed. What about:

STAR WARS

INDIANA JONES

THE BOURNE IDENTITY

LIKE WATER FOR CHOCOLATE

NO COUNTRY FOR OLD MEN

TOMMY BOY

TITANIC

THE AVENGERS

PRIDE AND PREJUDICE

They all follow the Field screenplay paradigm!

ACT 1: THE SETUP	ACT 2: THE CONFLICT	ACT 3: THE RESOLUTION
RELATABLE AND LIKABLE HERO	ENCOUNTERS ROADBLOCKS	BUT EMERGES TRANSFORMED

But how do we use this foundation for social selling, you may be asking yourself? Easy – we add the customer concentric aspect of storytelling:

ACT 1: THE SETUP	ACT 2: THE CONFLICT	ACT 3: THE RESOLUTION
RELATABLE AND LIKABLE HERO	ENCOUNTERS ROADBLOCKS	BUT EMERGES TRANSFORMED
CALL CUSTOMERS TO ATTENTION WHAT IS, AND WHAT COULD BE	CALL CUSTOMER TO ADVENTURE, SETTING THEM UP TO BE A HERO	CALL CUSTOMER TO ACTION, SO THEY CAN EMERGE TRANSFORMED

For Social Selling, the paradigm of GREAT STORIES is:

Act 1: Your relatable Hero (what you are selling) calls out to customers, grabbing their attention on what roadblocks are ahead, and that solutions (your product) exist.

Act 2: Clearly define roadblocks, with the promise of a solution; give them a sense that they can be the heroes in their own worlds if they just join you.

Act 3: Called to action, the customer emerges the New Hero, changing their own world with the help of your product.

Now your movie is taking form! Lets go back to the example once again of the children's retailer with the balanced, playful ONLY statement.

What does the Social Selling Movie Script look like in the context of creating GREAT STORIES for their base of influencers, peers, competitors and customers?

Children Outdoor Retailer
In an era when kids grow up to fast, one retailer realizes that parents ultimately want their kids to live balanced, playful lives. By eschewing the whims of fashion, they provide the highest quality outdoors apparel, and have created neighborhood environments that embrace and promote free activities with no connection to today's media and electronic based lives.

What a great story! What parent doesn't harken back (even if it's not true) to lives of yesteryear when kids ran free through the woods and fields, laughing and playing? What parent does not feel a bit guilty about not having the time to spend with their kids in our hectic, hectic times?

In this example, we see:

Act 1 – Our relatable Hero's (this time both kids and parents) realizes that they will have pressures of the modern world for their entire lives, but only will be kids once.

Act 2 – Technology and the lack of places and people who can provide a technology free experience is a roadblock. Luckily, our retailer steps in with a solution that will set our parents up to be heroes.

Act 3 – The parents take action, buying the retailer's quality outerwear, setting up outdoor activities, and taking advantage of the "walk in the woods" program that the retailer sponsors every Thursday for parents and kids. Both parents and kids emerge knowing they have changed. Parents are now letting their kids live a balanced and playful life, while the kids are no longer "connected" unwittingly to the completely techno-logical life.

TIME TO "ACT" OUT

Your homework is to write your movie!

Using the Field Paradigm, write your movie using the Act 1, 2 and 3 foundation. Ask yourself:

Act 1 (The Setup)

Who is the Hero for your story?
Is it you (yourself), or is it your product?

How is your Hero relatable?
Does what your selling solve a common problem? Does it make life easier for everyone? Does it make a long process significantly faster? Is the competition expensive, and you provide a cheaper solution?

How does your Hero show your customers what could be?
How, if they buy your product, will they feel better about themselves, grow stronger, loose less hair, beat their competitors, and sell more tables? If they join you on your journey (by buying from you) will they get promoted, save more money, age slower? Whatever the roadblock is, how does what you sell help overcome it?

Act 2 (The Conflict)

Have your clearly defined your customer Roadblock?
Has your customer had the "Ah Ha!" moment on how the Hero (you) have already identified what is causing them to "fail"?

Are there multiple conflicts that stand in the way?
If so, does what you are selling solve them all? If it solves the "biggest" issue easily, are you giving the customer a clear path to solve the rest?

Are you inviting the customer to resolve the conflict and be a Hero? Your story needs to show your customer how they can become the person who solves the issue so they feel good about themselves, good about their decision, and look good to others involved (like a boss or spouse!)

Act 3 (The Resolution)

Do you have a clear "Call to Action"?
Does your story have a way for the customer to "jump on board" (take action)? Is your Call to Action compelling, competitive and clear?

Is it as simple as "Yes" to take action?
If your customer simply has to say "yes", you have a compelling call to action. Try to make your promotion, sale, pitch, or process as clean and easy to understand as possible.

Does the resolution make the customer a Hero?
A compelling call to action, with a simple solution (saying "yes") that makes the customer a Hero is your direct path to success!

Now it's your turn – **WRITE YOUR MOVIE!**

As we lead our national clients through the process, we find people many times are instantly frozen with "writers block". Lets face it, being creative, and writing movie scripts is something few of us do in our daily lives. We have found the following steps helpful. Try it for yourself!

Think of your favorite movie. Now write a one-paragraph summary of it (as in the Horror Story example on page **125**).

Review your movie summary, and isolate whom the Hero's are, what the roadblock is, and how the Hero emerged transformed.

You're now in the creative mindset to write your own story.

Review your ONLY statement, and write your MOVIE summary just as you did for your favorite movie.

Isolate whom your Hero is, what roadblock you and your customers have, and how they will emerge transformed.

With your story in hand, go into a bit more detail for each ACT.

- Go into more detail about your Hero, and how you can engage them to see your product as a solution in Act 1.
- Define all aspects of the roadblock they have, and how your features and benefits solve the

roadblock, and why the competition does not in Act 2.
- Clearly define your "Call to Action" so that your customers can see themselves as the Hero as the resolve the roadblock in Act 3.

THAT'S IT! YOUR SCRIPT IS READY!

Now we'll let your story **LEAD** the way. Lets go!

"Seek, Learn, Grow...Or Fail" ™

Let us not look back in anger or forward in fear, but around in awareness.

- James Thurber

GREAT STORIES MAKE GREAT BLOCKBUSTERS

YOUR GUIDE TO G.R.E.A.T STORIES ARE: S.T.O.R.I.E.S

We learned as part of our FEED steps that to have a great "voice", you must be **G.R.E.A.T,** which means your content must be:

- **GENUINE**
- **RELATABLE**
- **ENTERTAINING**
- **AMAZING**
- **TRUSTWORTHY**

To LEAD and COMPEL, we need to combine what we have learned makes **G.R.E.A.T** content and apply it to the art of creating great stories, which are sincere, speak to a narrow and exact market, promise to provide a solution to a need, agree with your customers world perspective and have a distinct call to action.

Great stories, are S.T.O.R.I.E.S...

...where great stories have the following key elements or promises:

- **SINCERE**
- **TARGETED**

- **OATH**
- **REALITY**
- **IMPRESSIVE**
- **EMOTIONAL**
- **STIRRING**

SINCERE
Trusted. True. Sincere.

Your story needs to be from your heart. You'll be more successful at social selling when you believe in yourself, believe in what you are selling, and believe your own story. **Today, if any part of your MOVIE is fantasy, and therefore something you cannot deliver on, then it's not true and you'll quickly loose your customer's trust.**

TARGETED
Specific. Focused. Targeted.

Broad, wide-ranging, global stories (unless your story is a genuine "scoop") have little appeal, and have less chance of reaching your influencers and your customers. As legendary author Stephen Covey teaches in *"The 7 habits of highly effective people"*; Always Begin with the End in Mind. **Today, by narrowing and knowing your audience, you can broadcast your stories content to a focused group that are seeking your answer to their roadblock.**

OATH
Promise. Pact. Oath.

We should all live by the rule that a handshake means a promise kept. At all costs. Social selling should be based on the same high standard, and your story needs to have a promise inherent in it. The promise of less time spent on a mundane task. The promise of learning a language faster. The promise of more people attending a seminar. **Today, your story should promise and deliver on an Oath that you will resolve the conflict in the customer's life, allowing them to emerge triumphant.**

REALITY
Viewpoint. Perception. Reality.

Your story, since it is targeted at a narrow audience, must reflect their reality. You have little chance of changing their viewpoint with your story, but every chance of selling to them if your story agrees with their viewpoint. **Today, your customers need to see themselves as the Hero, feeling great about choosing your product, and reaffirming their viewpoint of the world.**

IMPRESSIVE
Exceptional. Different. Impressive.

The more you can deliver, the more impressive your OATH can be, the more the world will seek your solution. Brand wars are not won by matching the competition, they are won by adding one more feature, providing one more benefit, and offering more for less. Think outside the box, and make your story truly exceptional. **Today, if you deliver on your OATH, your IMPRESSIVE story will spread like wild fire!**

EMOTIONAL
Heart warming. Touching. Emotional.

The Hero (the customer) needs to have an emotional attachment to your story. They have to see themselves in your MOVIE, and see themselves as the Hero. They have to clearly see the resolution of thier conflict (using what your are selling) as the key part of emerging transformed. **Today, whether its getting the kudos of their boss, the love and admiration of their team, or the approval of their partner, your customer has to be emotionally tied to your product as their solution.**

STIRRING
Rousing. Compelling. Stirring.

Finally, your story must stir the soul and demand a call to action. Your customer must be so heavily attached to your story that they feel they have no choice but to do something – and that means purchase from you. Many of our greatest politicians have built life long careers on calling others to action. **Today, your story must end with a battle cry to action that compels your customers to say "yes".**

When you're done writing your story, review it with a critical eye to the S.T.O.R.I.E.S elements. Is it sincere and from your heart? Does it target a narrow, specific audience that will emotionally attach themselves to the exceptional promise you have made them? If so, then you have a great story that will compel them to action!

DON'T FORGET THE TRAILERS

Ok...so in our opinion there is nothing better than a good movie trailer. Trailers have all the elements of a great story boiled down to a few minutes, and end with the ultimate call to action - "Watch Me"! If you have ever been in the theater, watched a great trailer, and leaned over to whisper, "Boy, I want to see that when it comes out!" then you've experienced the ultimate in story telling. Think of the deep, baritone voice filling the theater for the trailers of our previous movie examples:

Horror Story
"Deep in a forgotten forest, where no one can hear you scream, stands a cabin with secrets that can't be let out. Ever."

Action Story
"Steve Smith retired from the CIA. Yesterday. Today, he only has to enlist the help of a rag-tag team of nefarious informants, and his wife, to save the world before sunset. He'll retire again tomorrow."

Love Story
"Don and Jackie are having the Paris honeymoon of their dreams. With other people. Their original promise many years ago to have and to hold, for better or worse, however seems to be coming true. What's worse than getting a divorce after 30 years? Falling in love again."

Well maybe we aren't the best trailer writers, but the point is simple. Great stories can be boiled down to catchy, quick and poignant punch lines – and yours can be to.

By creating a few "Trailers" for your MOVIE, you can tease your audience that great content is right around the corner.

As you'll see next, if you build your social selling platform on a great story, you can regularly build tension, suspense and interest in your social selling. What about our Children's retailer trailer? How about this:

Family Movie
"Perhaps the Milton kids greatest fear has just come true. Aunt Trudy is here, and everyone else is out. Literally, outside in the backyard."

Write your own **TRAILER** – and have fun!

You know what your problem is, it's that you haven't seen enough movies - all of life's riddles are answered in the movies.

- Steve Martin

The better I get, the more I realize how much better I can get.

- Martina Navratilova

LEAD STEP TWO:
OFFER COMPELLING PROMOTIONS

IT'S TIME FOR YOUR CLOSE-UP!

MAKE YOUR PROMOTIONS COMPELLING!

If your STORY is your right hook, then a great promotion is your secret left jab that will knock them out each time! Step two is to get your best promotions in place as you launch your GREAT STORIES.

HAVE A NEW PREMIER EVERY MONTH

In Hollywood, you can practically secure an invitation to a Premier every week. Just like we created your own MOVIE, the premier model is the entire movie making process in a nutshell.

- The trailers give us a taste of our story and get us excited.
- Advertising, social media, word-of-mouth, and reviews start infiltrating our conscious as the movie looms on the horizon.
- Tabloids, entertainment news, blogs and more broadcast pictures of the glamorous stars (the stories Hero's) on the red carpet.
- The Movie is released a crossed the nation, we flock to see it, and it becomes part of our own story. (We emerge transformed!)

You can use this same process to create excitement, buzz, and interest in what you are selling, by creating your own CALENDAR OF EVENTS for your premier each month (or as often as you want).

YOUR CALENDAR OF EVENTS

A Calendar of Events is simply a monthly calendar that lists the "cadence" of your social media, advertising, search engine optimization and email advertising endeavors' that support your story.

We have gathered several example calendar formats for your use. Take the time to visit

www.orfail.com/leadsteps

and view them.

You'll see, regardless of the format, they list the key steps to take during the days before your main event (the release of your story, or your compelling promotion).

The single biggest element of success among companies we have led, is their creation of (and use) of a Calendar of Events! Why?

A Calendar of Events keeps everyone on the same page. Literally. Your entire team knows when to take action to make your social selling efforts a success.

A Calendar of Events keeps you accountable. To really succeed at social selling, you have to have cadence and perseverance, taking the correct steps the same time, every time.

A Calendar of Events focuses your energies on your goal. No matter what you are selling, your goal is the same. Sell more! Your calendar will insure that all your efforts are spent on that goal.

And your Calendar of Events is the foundation for your next step – **creating compelling promotions!**

WHAT MAKES A GREAT PROMOTION?

Great promotions are not about you. They are about the customer, and the customer only.

Sure, done correctly you will reach your social selling goals to reduce your inventory, get that new job, or increase your visibility. But this simply means that you are using the basic elements of a great promotion to have reached them. These elements are:

Timely
Great promotions happen now. Not in the near future, not in the distant future. The easier it is for the customer to be rewarded for their decision to purchase, the more powerful. "**Save Now.**" "**Free Gift.**" "**10 Winners Every Day.**" Instant gratification is the keystone of powerful sales.

Promotions also gain more momentum and have more impact if they have a sense of urgency. Your call to action has to have a window of opportunity to have power. **"Ends Midnight Tonight."** **"2 Days Only."** **"Limited Time."** If your promotion has a clear sense of urgency, it motivates your customers' call to action.

Easy

Easy to understand, concise, and simple promotions are the most popular. Because consumers are hard-wired to make quick decisions in todays hectic culture, we gravitate towards the easiest to calculate and easiest to grasp. **"50% off."** **"Buy One Get One."** But ask a potential customer to calculate the savings of "Buy 1 Get 10%, Buy 2 Get 20% off the second, Buy 3 Get 30% off the third" and you'll get practically as many answers as the number of people you poll. Great Promotions are easy and understandable in the first 2 seconds.

Personal

Great promotions have to reward the customer, personally, the moment they decide to buy. A promotion that gives the purchaser a free product (gift with purchase) is the classic epitome of a promotion that becomes personal quickly. Have you ever asked yourself why department stores feature cosmetics and perfume in their most desirable space (right as you walk in the door?) Yes - it's a high profit area. But more importantly, this category was where the personal promotion was born.

**"Gift with purchase.""Buy One, get the Other Free."
"With every $50 purchase, get a $75 value bag for
only $20."** Personal promotions give your customer
the opportunity to keep something (the free perfume for example) and give the other as a gift. If your
promotion can be deeply personal by rewarding the
decision to purchase instantly, then you have a great
promotion.

Shareable
Sharing is the keystone of social selling. If your promotion either prompts your customer to share, or if
they are simply compelled to share it, then you'll have
a great promotion.

Within the social world, bloggers, forums and ecommerce sites pride themselves on delivering bargains,
deals and discounts to their followers. You can capi-
talize on this by rewarding sharing. One of the most
popular ways is to create a threshold based on reaching a milestone of sharing. For example, we offered
a 20% discount on any purchase if 2000 new people
signed up on the email list of a clothing website client. If 2500 signed up the discount for everyone (new
and old) would be 25%. The big push, however, was
to get over 5000 new customers signed up, and offer everyone 50% off. For the first few hours we were
tracking to barely make the 20% discount level. But
suddenly, as people finished dinner and the sense of
urgency to share (the promotion ended at midnight)
approached, we made and beat our 5000 new customer goal by several thousand!

Great promotions, like this one, are personal, timely, easy to understand, shareable - and fun!

Fun

Fun, energetic, humorous, and interesting campaigns gather the most momentum and catch our attention. Have fun with your campaigns! Think outside the box. One the best ways to find new ideas is to look well outside your own product or industry. First, look to the largest players, but then look at the up-start companies that are trying to take some of the big players market-share. That's where creative and fun promotions are being presented every day! Look at Coca-Cola or Pepsi, and then look at the regional soda maker, or the new coconut water drink, or the new energy drink. Look back to Apple and how they perfectly presented themselves as the new, creative and fun alternative to IBM as a up-start.

Have fun! Take risks! No regrets! These traits and this mindset make great promotions come to life!

COMPELLNG, PROVEN PROMOTIONS

Over the past 30 years, we have created hundreds of memorable and fun promotions for our companies and clients. The thrill of marketing is the energy surrounding the entire process of creating timely promotions that are personal and fun. Many of these quickly migrated from the physical world to the web for social selling. Others are unique to social selling and have gone the other way! Some of the proven promotions we have used, include:

Contests

"Enter to Win." These three words are more powerful and effective marketing tools than most people understand. It constantly amazes me how simple, and yet compelling, contests can be. A very large, national fast food chain customer of ours ran a contest to win an iPad. Millions of dollars were spent on in-store marketing, signage, entry forms, websites, and more. Their Facebook page tripled in "likes", their email list grew by hundreds of thousands of names, and nothing short of a viral buzz took place in the social world. And the grand prizes (10 were given away) cost only $600 each. Amazing.

Product Give-aways

Depending on what you are promoting, if you have the ability to offer product giveaways, by all means do it. Even if the product is you!

If you're selling low profit, high priced items it may be a harder strategy, but giving away your product, or promoting your product within a contest can be a great way to get visibility and gain market share.

One of the most clever giveaways we have seen was a business planner who offered a free day of her services as part of a contest to get leads. We followed up with her a few weeks after the winner had used her knowledge for a day (we didn't win) and found out she had been hired by the same firm for 6 months of full time work! Talk about a great strategy and investment on her part!

Customer Referrals

Customer referrals (harkening back to the "what we trust" section earlier) is what we believe. A great promotion can include rewarding those that refer others to your site. And the reward can be as creative as you are. Perhaps the more referrals a customer has, the more points they earn towards purchases in the future. Perhaps the more referrals they bring to you, the more they have access to exclusive promotions before others. Look to peers, competitors, and companies that you have referred to others to find inventive ways to promote customer referrals.

BOGA

BOGA is a term we use for "Buy One, Get Anything". The most popular BOGA program is "Buy One, Get One Free." "Buy One, Get One 50%" off is also incredibly powerful. We had the opportunity to play a part in the first apparel Buy One, Get One 50% off promotion in the US many, many years ago. Honestly, we "borrowed" it from a national shoe chain and our business grew at a staggering pace. BOGA promotions are timely, personal and easy, and are as powerful today as they were when introduced!

Gift with Purchase

Everyone loves a gift. Everyone loves getting something for free. Combined, a free gift with purchase is another powerful technique to promote your goods. If you sell multiple items of varying price ranges, an inexpensive item that is paired with a more expensive item suddenly has much more value. Getting two for the price of one, even if the free item is quite a bit less expensive than item that has to be purchased, is a compelling promotion.

We had a client with a severe overage in spectacularly made, beautiful leather jackets. Their customers historically cared little about price, but at over $1000 each, these jackets tested the limit of their comfort zone. At the same time, they had excess watches that retailed for $150 - $300, but cost only $20 - $40 to produce. Both of these products were guaranteed for life, and were items that the company knew their customers were be proud to own and proud to give away. You can see where this is going. We offered "the first 100 clients" a free watch of their choice (up to $300) with every purchase of the $1000 jacket. Not only did we sell every jacket in less than 3 hours, the company decided to order more jackets and run the promotion again every year thereafter!

Causes/Charities
Helping others, helping the community, and helping those in need is not only a great social obligation (in our opinion) but has created some of the most powerful promotional vehicles in modern marketing.
Lance Armstrong's iconic "Live Strong" yellow bracelet created an entirely new marketing tool now used by many other charities.

Certainly you run the risk of alienating some clients if you support a cause that has distinct opposition, but stick to your conviction and support the cause, or simply choose a cause that benefits everyone as it is furthered.

Surveys
"A penny for your thoughts? How about $25!" read the headline of our most successful online survey that not only gave us insight into how to improve our business and services, but delivered massive results. We offered $25 off the next purchase of $100 (a 25% discount) and we were rewarded with an overwhelmingly successful return rate.

Surveys, especially when paired with an incentive, are great promotions.

White Papers
We are all seeking knowledge – whether it's for work, for selling, for our personal life, or pleasure (hey – proof is that you're reading this right now!). A great way to speak to your area of expertise, and to promote your product, is by creating a white paper.

A white paper (which is a definitive report or guide that is usually helpful in solving a problem or issue) establishes your authority, allows you to speak to solutions for a problem, and helps individuals make a decision. Note that white papers should not overtly sell your solution, but you can insure the reader that you do have the product that will help them emerge transformed.

FREE (ANYTHING!)
Very few words are more powerful in marketing than "Free". We naturally associate savings, frugality, and intelligent purchasing decisions with something that is free. Similar to a BOGA promotion, anything that

can be given away Free (with no strings attached) will be a massive promotional tool for your business.

Don't overlook being creative with "Free" as well! You can give advice, time and problem solving away free just a much as you can dish washing soap or a tee shirt!

Opt In / Get More
Permission marketing (where marketers get permission to market to customers through the sales funnel) allows a closer relationship, and therefore more personal promotions specific to your customers needs. "Opting In" to your email and marketing efforts means that you have earned your customers trust, and interest. Reward this by promoting to these loyal customers first, giving them more access to discounted products and promotions.

"NARS" (Webinars, Seminars)
If your social selling efforts lend themselves to white paper promotions, then you may also want to consider creating a webinar or a seminar. Good webinars, however, need to deliver value, solutions and knowledge. Make sure you plan your webinar to be short but informative, well structured, and allow interaction with your audience.

SO, LEAD = COMPEL

COMPELLING STORIES ARE KEY IN TODAYS RIGHT BRAIN WORLD

THE MOST COMPELLING STORY IS YOURS

YOUR STORY HAS A RELATABLE HERO, WHO OVER-COMES A ROADBLOCK, AND EMERGES TRANSFORMED.

YOUR ONLY STATEMENT BECOMES YOUR MOVIES ACT 1, 2, AND 3

GREAT STORIES ARE SINCERE, TARGETED, HAVE AN OATH OR A PROMISE, ARE BASED IN YOUR CUSTOM-ERS REALITY, AND IMPRESSIVE AND HAVE A STIRRING CALL TO ACTION.

COMBINE YOUR G.R.E.A.T CONTENT AND YOUR GREAT S.T.O.R.I.E.S FOR SOCIAL SELLING SUCCESS!

"

Success seems to be connected with action. Successful people keep moving. They make mistakess but they never quit.

- Conrad Hilton

LEAD STEP THREE:
COMPEL WITH THE RIGHT TOOLS

HERES THE BEST TOOLS TO LEAD TODAY.

New tools to help with content, story creation, or just plain inspiration when you need it, are coming online each day, so make sure you check at

www.orfail.com/leadtools

for updates.

TOOLS TO HELP WRITE YOUR STORY

A great way to hone your story, and to continue to deliver great content, is to find great story sites. Try these:

STORIFY YOUR STORY

Storify.com "...helps its users tell stories by curating social media." We are fans' of their easy to access content, inspirational ideas, and the wide variety of stories to build off of.

www.storify.com

Storify creates the story layer above social networks,

helping to amplify influential users within your category. In essence, they have created a usable, new platform for the story aspect of your social selling efforts.

GET YOUR STORYFUL

Storyful has teams of professional journalists creating and curating (separating real news from fluff) around the clock.

www.storyful.com

They offer a free trial, and free access to a tremendous library of content. It's a great place to "learn from the best" when creating your story and your content. We particularly like their "storybuilder" tool to develop compelling stories. Give it a try!

YOUR PAPER.LI PAPER

It's worth taking time to visit Paper.li, a site devoted to helping create your own online newspaper. Not only a good addition to your social selling efforts, we often use Paper.li to stimulate the story creating process.

www.paper.li

If your audience likes up to the minute information, then using Paper.li may help you publish a newspaper based on topics they like, and help you deliver fresh news, daily.

SU, SU, SULIA

Sulia is a hybrid between a social network and an influencer gathering site – with free access to content as well.

www.sulia.com

Sulia connects trusted sources and content enthusiasts on thousands of subjects, using a combination of network managers and sophisticated algorithms to identify the best-regarded sources across thousands of topics. The result is streams of content we have found to be on-topic, readable, and relevant.

FLIP OUT OVER FLIPBOARD

Flipboard is a good example a new content curating sites (Zite and Google Currents being others to review) that study your reading habits and provide articles, blogs, tweets and other content tailored to your interests.

www.flipboard.com

Flipboard uses a very easy, simple layout that allows for quick "sampling" of content and articles, as well as the ability to dig deeper into the subject if you want. Flipboard is great for mobile content reviewing as well.

TOOLS TO FIND COMPELLING PROMOTIONS

Compelling promotions flourish on the web. Sometimes, however, you may need help digging up the visionary juices, finding the right promotion, or knowing if it will work. Following are sites that provide expert advice, insight and ideas on how to make compelling promotions.

JUMP INTO THE MARKETING ZONE

MarketingZone is a great, free resource with practically unlimited access to great marketing and promotional ideas.

www.marketingzone.com

It's also a great content site as well, with access (although you have to pay for it) to experts in hundreds of industries that can answer specific questions. We particularly find their free small business and social media guides section helpful.

ASK THE PROFS

MarketingProfs is a community of nearly 500,000 small business owners, entrepreneurs and professional marketers who have gathered to create a library of newsletters, articles, podcasts and guides.

www.marketingprofs.com

They offer both a free membership and a paid version with access to additional information.

MAGAZINE SITES

Many of our most popular business magazines offer free access to an amazing about of marketing and promotional materials.

www.inc.com
www.fastcompany.com
www.forbes.com
www.businessweek.com
www.entrepreneur.com

None of the magazine sites require a subscription to access, but several allow access to up to the minute data, or to large archives if you are a subscriber.

WE ARE A START UP NATION

StartUpNation is a free site that gathers those who are thinking of starting a business, those we are in the midst of the process, and those who have done so successfully.

www.startupnation.com

READY TO MEASURE SUCCESS OF YOUR SOCIAL SELLING?

The things that get measured are the things that get done.

- Michael Labeouf

PART SIX

MEASURE YOUR SUCCESS WITH SOCIAL SELLING METRICS

UNDERSTAND THE BEST METRICS TO USE

American management guru Peter Drucker created many of our business cultures most important constructs. As early as 1959, in his pioneering book *"The Landmarks of Tomorrow"*, Drucker described the significant change that was happening in the workplace in the United States, and the world. His introduction of the "knowledge worker" concept was one of the first acknowledgements that we were shifting from a manufacturing economy, to what he termed "the information economy."

Even in these early times, decades before a world wide web that connects a global infrastructure, Drucker and others knew that measurement techniques and tools created for the manufacturing of goods could be reconstructed and applied to the an information dependent world. Drucker's vision has come true, and can be applied to your social selling efforts.

Social media metrics, because of the pioneering works of those like John Lovett's *"Social Media Metrics Secrets"* and Jim Sterne's *"Social Media Metrics"*, have advanced at lightening speed in the last few years.

At the same time, tools and techniques for measuring success have become readily available.

Even with these advances, however, lets take a moment to acknowledge there are limitations.

A WARNING ABOUT SOCIAL SELLING METRICS

Social Selling Metrics are not 1+1=2

They are more like 1+1=1.78

For those of us who like linear, sharp and clean metrics (we will lump ourselves into this group as well), we're not quite "there" in the art and science of social media or social selling metrics.

Yet.

John Lovett, metrics expert and co-founder of consulting firm Web Metrics Demystified (which is also the name of their firms book) admits, *"Confusion and Bewilderment are common emotions evoked in businesses working to understand (social metrics)."*

The key, however, to "demystifying" the process, is to

use metrics, performance indicators, or goals that are based on easy to gather data, and easy to understand components that create easy to act on results.

That's where the **S.M.A.R.T** methodology helps! Let see!

FIRST, USE S.M.A.R.T METRICS

SMART is a common mnemonic originally introduced into American business vernacular in the early 1980's as a way to define a meaningful set of KPI (Key Performance Indicators, or goals) standards.

For our purposes, we'll make sure using the S.M.A.R.T methodology applies to the appropriate social selling metrics. They are:

- **SIMPLE**
- **MEASURABLE**
- **ACHIEVALBE**
- **RELEVANT**
- **TIIMELY**

Simple
Social Selling Metrics have to be clear, simple and easy to understand. The more complex the metric, the harder it will be to get others to "be on board" with the metric as a way of reviewing performance.

Measurable
Goals that are practically immeasurable, or even difficult to measure, will be a headache every time you try to review results. Make sure you clearly define what the components of data you need for your goals, and have an easy way to get to the data.

Note that getting to data doesn't have to "be pretty" to be effective. Sometimes, it's just as simple to write everything down on a piece of paper to calculate results, as it is to find a systemic way to get results.

(That being said, all the metrics we will discuss in our Top 10, are easy to access through online tools!)

Achievable
SMART goals must be achievable. You'll set yourself up for failure and frustration if your goals are "over the moon" from the moment you start.

Make small realistic goals. Day by day, then week by week at first. As you become more of an expert in social selling, (and you begin to flex your own influence), then you can start to create more aggressive goals.

Goals that can be achieved, goals that can come true, will get you (and your teams) confidence up in order to meet and beat the Big Goals you have for the future!

Relevant
Your Social Selling goals have to mean something. A goal such as "create an easy to read blog" may be achievable, but is not very relevant. If, on the other

had, your goal is "Create an easy to read blog that grows by 10% a month for the first 10 months"; you have a relevant goal that will lay the foundation for your social selling efforts.

Make sure your goals are relevant to the individuals that are getting them done, as well. Overall goals are a great way to motivate everyone involved, but make sure that everyone has goals specific to their challenges and responsibilities that directly contribute to your Big Picture.

Timely
SMART goals are timely, and have an end date. In this sense, timely means they can be measured at a certain point in time. Maybe it's every day, or every week. Maybe it's only at the end of the month, but more likely (in the fast paced social selling world we live in) you'll have access to your metrics 24 hours a day, 7 days a week.

Wrap your goals into a larger time frame as well, with smaller goals leading up to a large goal. Set 6 month or annual goals that are an aggregate of your daily, weekly and monthly goals. With a larger goal firmly set on the horizon, you'll always know how every action you take is effecting your bigger goal, and you'll be able to constantly evaluate your progress and make any necessary changes to your plan if needed.

So what SMART Social Selling metrics should you use?

It's easy. Use the Top 10!

Ready to Measure? Lets go!

THE TOP 10 SOCIAL SELLING METRICS (OK, 9)

Hundreds of Social Selling Metrics have been created recently, and many more are being created everyday.

Below are the Top 10 metrics (collectively agreed upon by industry experts) that closely follow the SMART construct.

Ok, so you probably noticed there are only 9 goals, but you'll see the method to our madness after we take a quick look at the definitions and components of each metric. They are:

Interaction
Interaction is the amount of interest your specific campaign or individual social selling effort call to action generates.

Interaction = Conversions/Activity

Engagement
Engagement is the degree of which customers interact with your specific campaign or social selling effort. It's a way of gaging the depth in which customers are interacting with your initiative.

Engagement = Visits x Time x Comments x Shares

Influence
Influence (as we have talked about through out this book) is one of the most powerful components of successful social selling. It is the power to compel others to take action.

Influence = Volume of Relevant Content x Comments x Shares x Reach

Share of Voice
Share of Voice is your "market share" of total ongoing discussions within your industries peers, competitors and brands. It's a great way to understand, over time, how much your influence is effecting your overall positioning in the market.

Share of Voice = Brand Mentions / Total Mentions (Your Brand + Brand B + Brand C + etc...)

Page Views
The number of Page Views is perhaps the easiest metric to gather and is readily available from your hosting provider, your blog platform, or from Google Analytics. It is simply the number of individuals who visited, and viewed, your online undertakings.

Page Views = Number of Visitors for Each Page

Conversion
Conversion rate is the total number of "closes" or "sales" you have for each social selling effort or campaign. It's

a great way to gage the impact of your call to action because it delivers the number of individuals who actually follow through on it.

Conversion = Total # of Completed Transactions / Total Engaged Audience

Advocates

Advocates measures the individuals (outside of your own efforts) who are supporting your social selling efforts. Advocates themselves deliver enthusiasm, positive support, and are evangelical about who you are, and what you are doing.

Advocates = Influence x Positive Comments

Impact

Impact measures the ability to guide the outcome of your social selling effort or campaign. Impact is a good metric to use for your efforts, or applied to social media network, a blog, a forum or the like.

Impact = Outcomes / (Interactions+Engagement)

Reach

Reach provides you an understanding of the size of the audience you're marketing to. It's a great metric to see the overall marketing potential you have for your social selling efforts.

Reach = Seed Audience x Shared Network Audience

METRICS AND YOUR SALES FUNNEL

It's worth taking a moment to connect two concepts we have discussed so far: Your sales funnel and metrics.

Metrics, regardless of which you choose, give you insight into how your customers are interacting within your sales funnel. When you've decided which metrics are important to you, take the time to know where they apply to your sales funnel, and where you can best react to what you learn from them!

WHICH METRICS? IT'S AS EASY AT TICK, TACK, TRACK!

So which metrics do you start with?

All of them? Sure, but...

...it might be a bit overwhelming to set up, understand, rally behind, and track all of these metrics. We like to introduce metrics to our clients using a tool we have developed over the years.

We call it "**Tick, Tack, Track.**" We've arranged the Top 9 (see why its 9, not 10 now!) key metrics into a simple Tic Tac Toe chart, insuring that no matter which you way you connect three metrics, you'll have a good basis to start from!

So time to play! Simply review the definitions earlier, so you have a good understanding of each metric, then, connect a Tic Tac Toe line of any three and you'll have your social selling metrics to begin with!

INTERACTION	ENGAGEMENT	INFLUENCE
SHARE OF VOICE	PAGE VIEWS	CONVERSION
ADVOCATES	IMPACT	REACH

In God we trust, all others bring data.

- W. Edwards Deming

BEST SOCIAL SELLING METRIC TOOLS

Tools abound to measure your social selling efforts, and many are free. As always, we'll keep you updated on what we believe to be the best tools at

www.orfail.com/metrictools

METRIC TOOLS

THE 800-POUND "GOOGRUILLEA"

Free and powerful. That's the best way to describe Google Analytics. If you have to choose one tool for your efforts (although we suggest using several), Google Analytics should probably be it.

www.google.com/analytics/

You'll also want to hone up on your Google analytics skills for future mobile efforts as well.

GIVE A HOOT. THEY DO.

We're fans of Hootsuite, and endorsed them earlier as well. Hootsuite has provided a robust set of metric measuring tools in an easy to use format. Check out this feature at:

www.hootsuite.com/features/custom-analytics

THE <u>OTHER</u> 800-POUND GUIRELLA

No list of metric providers would be complete without mentioning Facebook's own social media metric and analysis tool – Insights. It's an easy to install and use tool that gives you tremendous access to data about your Facebook efforts. Find more at:

https://developers.facebook.com/docs/insights/

A TREAT FOR TWEETING

Tweetgrader is an easy to use, free twitter metric tool from HubSpot. We've endorsed HubSpot in earlier chapters, and give them a thumbs-up here as well. You can get a quick twitter score of influence, or jump into the many other tools they provide for more in-depth metric reviews.

www.tweet.grader.com

GET A BOOST FROM CROWDBOOSTER

Crowdbooster currently offers analytics only for Twitter and Facebook, but we hope they expand their scope soon. They provide a dashboard of metrics, as well as give recommended actions based on your efforts in order to improve on each metric.

www.crowdbooster.com

BE A MOVER AND A BOOSHAKA

Booshaka is a newer player in the field, offering a platform from start to finish for both metrics and social strategy – a process they call "Understand, Engage, and Amplify". They have a free option, and then reasonably priced upgrades as your needs grow.

www.booshaka.com

LET YOUR SOCIAL EFFORTS SPROUT

As early users of sproutsocial, we've used it now for longer than most, and have not been disappointed. Sproutsocial integrates more networks than most (Twitter, Facebook, LinkedIn and more) and creates a single place for measuring your social selling efforts.

www.sproutsocial.com

GET YOUR SOCIAL REPORT CARD

SocialReport offers a free trial for their analytics solution that they describe as "Google Analytics for Social Networks". It allows for tracking of many of the key metrics on the Tick, Tack, Track chart as well as allowing you to track visitors, time on site, keywords, geography and many other aspects of web performance.

They report on a wide variety of data, including any membership information you may have, demographics, interests, customer geography, educational efforts, employment history, and many other aspects of your social space.

www.socialreport.com

WE MUST MENTION SOCIAL MENTION

SocialMention is a great listening tool that aggregates content from across the universe into a single stream of information, allowing you to track and measure what people are saying about you and your product – in real time. They monitor hundreds of social networks, and have created a free, powerful tool for your social selling efforts.

www.socialmention.com

"Seek, Learn, Grow...Or Fail" ™

If you have no idea where you want to go, it makes little difference how fast you travel.

- Italian Proverb

PART SEVEN

WHAT YOU WANT...IS WANT

Everyone is selling something people **want.**

Social buttons (the most famous being the Facebook Like button) changed social networking, and are changing social selling as well.

Actually, "changing" is not a powerful enough word. More aptly said, social selling is about to be revolutionized, and you'll **WANT** to be part of it.

First, lets look at how we got to the revolution.

A BIT OF LIKE HISTORY

Winston Churchill said, "Victory is written by the victors", and perhaps the history of the "Like" button is one of greatest twenty first century examples.

You'll find varied stories on how it came to be, and who started the concept of collecting desire-based data, but for our purposes we'll follow the victor's recollection, as detailed by Facebook insider and Director of Engineering Andrew 'Boz' Bosworth, who was part of a small group who worked on the project, code-named "Props".

In mid July of 2007, a group of 5 Facebook employees begin discussions on the concept of a button that could allow as user to express their like, enjoyment, and support of certain content. They threw around the idea of a star rated system (like used in reviews), a plus sign, or even a "thumbs up" icon. They temporarily agreed on "awesome" as the working name.

Only 4 days after their discussion, the group produced a working prototype of the "awesome" button, and work on creating the platform began. Renamed "Like" through the process, the project received only a lukewarm response from Facebook founder Mark Zuckerberg, even through their competitor Friendfeed introduced their own "like" button before Facebook did. Zuckerberg's concern was the possible confusion and cannibalization of the Facebook "share" feature.

Over the next year and a few months, Facebook tested the concept of the Like button in News feeds and Advertising, finally launching "Like" in February of 2009.

And the social world, as well as social selling, was changed forever.

Currently, as we end 2012, there are nearly 1 million Facebook Likes every minute, and over 1.3 billion Likes every day. If you combine both Comments and Likes, you have over 2.1 million Likes and Comments every hour, and over 3 billion every day.

And with millions upon millions of sites featuring Like functionality, whether its to sign up, to show support, or to gain recognition, it's easy to make the case that Facebook changed social media forever with the Like button.

And they just did it again.

NOT EVOLUTION, BUT REVOLTION: WANT

It was enterprising blogger Tom Waddington who first discovered Facebook's intent to create a much more robust e-commerce platform when he found they had added hidden software code within their developer site in June of 2012.

This code clearly created the ability for users to "Want" an item, in the same manor that they could "Like" an item.

Creating quite a stir by those who saw the power of this protocol, Facebook simply at the time stated *"We're always testing new Platform features, however we have nothing new to announce."*

It was several months later, in October of 2012 that Facebook officially launched its test of "Facebook Collections", and the introduction of both their "Want" button and the "Wish List" platform it created.

With the help of 7 carefully selected retailers (most notably Victoria's Secret, Pottery Barn and online rising star Fab.com) the Facebook Collections test allowed users to curate and publish wish lists similar to Pinterest's visual format. Friends could then click on any item from this "photo album" and purchase directly from the retailer's site.

Facebook tested several button options – including "Want" and "Collect", (and even "Like") in order to determine which button description was the most successful. Clicking on the button then posted a picture of that item to a section of the users timeline called "Products" or "Wish lists". Facebook also tested whether these Products or Wish lists would be visible only to friends, or to friends of friends.

The test lasted only a few weeks, and many industry pundits thought it might have been unsuccessful.

The truth is, that much like the success of the Like platform, the Want platform was successful enough to warrant putting the might and resources of Facebook into full action.

As of this publishing, fresh after their tests success, we believe Facebook is proceeding with improvements from what they learned to enhance the user experience, create a mobile version, and push for a massive launch of their product quickly.

How can we be so confident that Facebook will move forward with their Collect or Want platform? We just need to look to proven successes in the same venue to see the power of Want.

THE POWER OF WANT

It's Full Disclosure time. We had a gut level belief in the power of the Want protocol well before it was part of the Facebook discussions. One of our largest clients, Fredericks of Hollywood (number 321 on Internet Retailers Top 500 list) tested the Want button concept using software developed by a third party provider.

It was during part of this test that we realized the sheer potential of the "Want" or "Collect" concept for social selling. As a publically traded company, we cannot disclose any data about the test, but we can say that we quickly implemented it a crossed the wide variety of retail clients we have the honor of serving.

Certainly other online companies and networks have created similar products.

Third party vendors such as WANT (funded by the always savvy Camelot Venture Group) introduced versions, as well as Froomerce, 8th Bridge and the network Shopify.

Lest we forget our forefathers, Amazon pioneered the wish list concept within their own digital bounds, and broke free soon after – giving shoppers the ability to add products from any site to their personal list.

So how are Facebook's efforts so different than those before it? It's the combination of a proven path to success forged by its Like button, and its over 1 billion users eager to engage with people and products, that create the perfect social selling storm to create a revolution, not evolution, unlike we have seen before.

So what's in it for you and your social selling?

Everything!

STILL NEED A REASON TO PUT THE POWER OF WANT TO WORK FOR YOU?

HOW ABOUT 10!

There's a bunch of reasons why the Like platform has been so successful, and why the Want or Collect platform will be even bigger for social selling.

Lets look at the Top 10 reasons why Want will change selling forever.

10. Exclusivity
Think Facebook exclusive products, and Facebook only offers. By gathering everyone that Wants your item onto one part of the social sales funnel, you'll have a captive audience who has already pledged their allegiance to being first in line for discounts, limited editions, and colors or styles only available if they Want your brand, product or page.

9. A Universal Wish List
Blogger David Clarke wrote of the Want platform. *"Think of it as a wish list on steroids."* With its scope and breadth, and with a few key alliances (such as Amazon), the Want protocol creates a worldwide wish list. Since 30% of all online purchases start with Amazon – imagine the power of the 1,2 punch the Want button will create.

8. One Stop Shopping
Facebook could completely rethink the social shop-

ping (and shopping experience for that matter!) by creating a one stop shopping platform. For example, if a user "Wants" an item, they could be led to a Google Shopping or Amazon style single sourcing page that lists the top competitors, pricing and offers for that item – reducing time searching for deal dramatically for many online consumers.

7. Increased Exposure
Envision the increased exposure the Want platform could deliver for your product, yourself or your cause. Lets say you have decided to sell tee shirts for your upcoming Breast Cancer Awareness campaign. Doug wants to support you, so he clicks on the Want button and purchases. Almost instantly his timeline is updated, and Sally see's the tee shirt, and she buys as well.

All of their friends have seen the purchase, and their friends, etc....now that's exposure!

6. The power of what we don't know
Never underestimate the creativity of social people, who will find ways to use Want in ways we have not even thought of yet. Did we think that the Like platform would create an entirely new way to market? Not really. Did we know it would be one of the most powerful ways to run contests on the web? Nope. Did we think it would become a defacto way to register for many online activities? Nada.

With the power of Want, we'll see an even bigger emphasis on creative uses!

5. Cross Selling

If you sold tennis balls, how much would you pay to know instantly (in real time?) who had just bought an expensive tennis racquet?

Or perhaps you sell robotic vacuum cleaners that scurry about the floor while you're at work. How much would you love to know everyone that just told the world they wanted recycled barn wood flooring?

The Want platform creates an entirely new, and more powerful, cross-selling platform.

4. Efficient

Morris Hite said, *"Advertising is salesmanship mass produced."* For decades, salesmanship was thrown out to the masses in the hopes to catch enough interest to justify the cost. With online advertising, we took a massive step towards narrowing our sales pitches to a more interested audience – those searching for something at least close to what we are selling.

Want protocol will be a revolutionary step forward in salesmanship, providing us with people who have already informed us they are interested and Want our product. Advertising budgets will be spent more effectively, and on customers who are already well into the social selling sales funnel.

3. Visual

By the nature of how Facebook has tested and envisioned the use of the Want button, it's a very visual platform. The more visual your selling efforts are, the more you can "tell a thousand words with a picture", the greater opportunity the Want button will present for you.

You only need to know a bit about Pinterest to see how successful the concept of visual curating can be:

- 80% of the Pins (users choosing content to share) on Pinterest are repins (sharing with others), while only 1.4% of Tweets are reTweeted on Twitter!

- Pinterest has grown as fast as 53% in one month! And, from mid 2011 to mid 2012, Pinterest had grown by 2700%!

- Pinterest is now more powerful than Twitter for referral traffic for social selling!

- The average order size of a sale that came from Pinterest is over $80, double that of Facebook, and even higher than Amazon!

- Shopify.com saw the number of orders generated from Pins quadruple in the first half of 2012!

So if Facebook continues to provide a Pinterest similar look and feel, there is little reason to doubt the visual aspect of the platform could be incredibly powerful.

2. Intention
The Want buttons shows intent to purchase, the holy grail of advertising. The customer has enough intent,

enough vested interest in what you are selling, to tell the world they want it!

Here's where the power of the want button cuts through the entire sales funnel process and lands us squarely between Desire and Action. (Time to go back and look at the New Social Sales Funnel!) We know we have their Attention and certainly know we have their Intention. Now its up to us to convert Desire into Action!

And that's why the number one reason to Want the Want button is...

1. Entirely New Promotional Platform
Rarely, in the world of marketing and promotion, are entirely new platforms created.

1704 – Newspaper advertising appears
1742 – First magazine ads
1920 – First radio sponsors appear
1941 – First Television ads are shown
1993 – Online advertising is born

So is 2013 the next Big Step? Probably.

Let's look at an example of the power of the Want button for what we'll call *CrowdSaving*. Social sellers will be able to aggregate those who Want a product and offer discounts for the more people that come on board. Perhaps a 10% discount for 100 people, but a 30% discount if 1000 people want the product.

Could this new "CrowdSaving" platform be a Groupon Killer platform? What's the need for Groupon if everyone can come together at the click of a button and easily demand a large reduction or deal on a product with virtually no effort on their part?

We'll be able to use this entirely new platform, full of rich, social desire based data, to make efficient advertising decisions in order to reach customers who already have jumped into the key social selling zone of the sales funnel!

Now that's a whole new world!

But, you're probably asking yourself why go on and on about something that's not quite available yet.

The answer is that your timing is perfect!

Prepare now and you'll be ahead of your peers, and your competition.

Here's how…

WHAT TO DO NOW

So how do you add the Want platform to your social selling efforts now? Well, just by acknowledging it, and by learning about it, you can take the simple steps shown below to be ahead of everyone.

Be an early adopter

Follow progress on the launch of the Want or Collect platform and sign up for it as soon as Facebook launches its updated Collections functionality.

To do this, create a Google Alert similar to "Facebook Want Button", and you'll be kept in the loop at least daily on Facebook's progress.

Try a third party option

By all means, you can build the foundations of your Want strategy using one of several third party Want Buttons already offered.

As we noted earlier, we have experience with several, and have found that we are significantly ahead of our competition by being an early adopter using third party products.

Use existing social network buttons

If you haven't used the Facebook Like platform, get to know it inside and out. Chances are the Want process will be very similar in use and execution.

At the same time, try out Facebook's Gift protocols and make yourself familiar with its process, use and objectives.

Other networks use protocols as well. Try Twitters Like option, Google's +1 buttons, and of course know Amazons Wish process.

Know Pinterest
Since Pinterest is a proven social network to drive sales, certainly make it part of your current social selling efforts if you think the Want platform could be powerful for you in the future. By getting familiar with Pinterest, you'll be creating a great knowledge base to get a jump on the competition in the near future!

You can be the next leader!
Flex your creative muscles now! Think of great promotions that will translate in the World of the Want button and try them now. By "working out the kinks" of new and creative promotions, you'll be that much better prepared to take advantage of the Want platform when it's launched.

Immerse yourself in books about advertising and social selling, subscribe to blogs about marketing, and join forums on promotions.

Take this time, **the calm before the storm**, to re-imagine your business as a leader in social selling. Create a new vision for yourself, and what you are selling. Think of this new phase of amazing technological journey as your opportunity to re-think, re-energize and re-launch yourself as tomorrow's social selling leader!

Maybe the best way to define your future is to reinvent it.

- George Lois

FINAL THOUGHTS

First, congratulations are in order!

YOU DID IT!

We hope that this OR FAIL book gives you better sense of the importance of social selling, and how it can radically improve your business and your life.

At the same time, we hope that the style, format and simplicity of the OR FAIL series truly did impact your life for the better, and that our easy to follow steps have given you the insight and confidence to get the job done – whether you're jumping into social selling to help with a simply project, or change the entire way you manage day to day.

We think you deserve some recognition, by the way! Log onto **www.ORFAIL.com** and print out your free Certificate of Education. At the same time, we have links to lots and lots of additional resources for furthering your education.

THE GLOVES ARE OFF! AN OPEN CHALLENGE FOR DUMMIES AND COMPLETE IDIOTS.

We are so confident that the radically simple approach of our OR FAIL series is a faster, better way to learn that we challenge any Dummies® and Complete Idiot® titles on an identical subject we publish. Here's our challenge:

"If you read a Dummies® or Complete Idiot® on the same subject of any OR FAIL title and you believe you have learned more from their titles, we will refund the complete price of your OR FAIL purchase."

100% GUARANTEED.

At the same time, let us know what you liked better about the competitions title. It will help make our OR FAIL series better in the long run!

Go to **www.ORFAIL.COM/CHALLENGE** for more.

Dummies® is registered mark of Wiley Publishing. Complete Idiot® is registered mark of Penguin Publishing.

"Seek, Learn, Grow...Or Fail" ™

ACKNOWLEDGEMENTS

So many people came together to make this book possible.

First and foremost, I want to thank Neethy, Priya and Rory – who supported every aspect of all my projects, crazy ideas, and tangents. Specifically the support of my wife, Neethy, has given more than I deserve for the last 30 years.

Jonathan Roberts – life long friend from which abundance, intelligence, humility and humor seems to radiate from. Without his influence and support, making this a reality would not have happened.

Troy Larson – finding family after 25 years is a treasure! Thanks for the help, and here we go!

And finally to Bryan Krieger – your encouragement and intelligence made this project a reality.

ABOUT THE AUTHOR

Garr Larson has over 25 years of executive, marketing, management, and ecommerce experience working with many of the nations largest retail brands.

He was a founding executive of Hot Topic, one of the nations largest teen retailers, has been President and CEO of several national retailers, and is CMO of Transformworks, Inc.

He lives in Santa Monica, CA with his family and a high maintenance dog.

ABOUT THE CREATIVE DIRECTOR

Troy Larson is a renowned graphic artist and designer, with clients at all corners of the world. Troy's award winning work includes logo development, periodical production, and web development for many national and international clients.

WANT TO WRITE FOR OR FAIL?

Are you an expert in your field and want to pitch us a title you'd like to write for the OR FAIL series?

DO IT!

Send us your bio and the topic you have a passion for. There is a chance we have already selected or begun a similar title (great minds think alike!), but lets connect anyway. Go to: **www.orfail.com/authorinfo**

But remember: Rewards come after you complete your manuscript (no up front payments)

It's a long, hard process that most do not finish.

We're a small publishing firm, but fun to work with, and we ask a lot of our authors. Still...

It could change your life!